Neue Nationalgalerie
Mies van der Rohe's Museum

Ludwig Mies van der Rohe on the day of the raising of
the roof of the Neue Nationalgalerie, April 5, 1967

Neue Nationalgalerie

Mies van der Rohe's Museum

For the Nationalgalerie, Staatliche Museen zu Berlin,
edited by Joachim Jäger and Constanze von Marlin

With photographs by Simon Menges

Deutscher Kunstverlag

Nationalgalerie
Staatliche Museen zu Berlin

Forewords

The Neue Nationalgalerie, which was built between 1963 and 1968, as the last project planned by Ludwig Mies van der Rohe that he was able to implement himself, is considered to be this important architect's great legacy. With its transparent glass hall above and free wall placements on the collection floor below, this building embodies the idea of the open spatial layout that Mies van der Rohe pursued from the 1920s onward. The Neue Nationalgalerie building thus stands at the end of a long line of development ranging from Mies's early brick country house of 1924, by way of his legendary German Pavilion for the 1929 International Exposition in Barcelona, to the large steel-and-glass buildings of his Chicago period.

For Berlin, the building was at once a form of amends to the former director of the Bauhaus, who had immigrated to Chicago because he lacked the freedom and opportunity to work after the National Socialists closed the Bauhaus in 1933. At Berlin's invitation, Mies van der Rohe returned in the early 1960s to begin planning the Neue Nationalgalerie. What good fortune for this city!

The "temple of Western modernism" that he conceived is one of the most beautiful and impressive museum buildings of the twentieth century. After nearly fifty years of constant use, however, an extensive restoration could be postponed no longer. In David Chipperfield Architects, we found architects who preserved the legacy of Mies in a unique way, while nevertheless managing to update the building for modern museum operations. The focus of the entire restoration was the ceaseless balancing of interests between preserving the existing structure and using the building as a modern institution for collecting and exhibiting. The result speaks for itself. David Chipperfield Architects has once again—as it had with the Neues Museum (New Museum) on the Museumsinsel (Museum Island)—set standards for dealing with historical buildings.

The present volume is dedicated to all facets of the building—from the process of constructing it to the opening phase that was so important for Berlin and Germany to the present day. Brilliant series of photographs by Simon Menges document the restoration that was so respectful of Mies and offer a new perspective on this iconic building. In their diverse contributions, prominent authors circle around the myth of this special building, which numbers among the highlights not just of Berlin but also of the Stiftung Preussischer Kulturbesitz (Prussian Cultural Heritage Foundation).

Hermann Parzinger
President of the Stiftung Preussischer Kulturbesitz

"Galerie des 20. Jahrhunderts" (Gallery of the Twentieth Century) was still written on the plans by Ludwig Mies van der Rohe, before the building, shortly prior to its opening, was given its final name: Neue Nationalgalerie. Today the building is still dedicated to the art of the twentieth century. The combined collection of the State of Berlin and the Stiftung Preussischer Kulturbesitz (Prussian Cultural Heritage Foundation), which was merged in 1967 in what was then West Berlin, had a broad span from the art of the early nineteenth century to contemporary art. When designing the spaces for the collection, Mies van der Rohe had been inspired by the collection of the Museum of Modern Art in New York and created especially well balanced rooms with a ceiling height of 4 meters, which was indeed very generous for the circumstances of the time but not oversized.

The Neue Nationalgalerie is unique not only for the elegance with which Mies van der Rohe solved the two briefs for the museum—namely, creating both a large space for special exhibitions and rooms for the collection—by dividing these two functions onto two floors. The Neue Nationalgalerie is famous above all for the openness of the hall and the open layout of the spaces on the floor for the collection. Although some critics considered the glass hall unfeasible at the opening in 1968, its potentials have been developed fully in the nearly fifty years of its exhibition history. A detailed appreciation is offered by the volume *Die Ausstellungen: Neue Nationalgalerie, 1968–2015,* which was published in 2018.

With the reopening of the Neue Nationalgalerie after its comprehensive renovation, a new era begins. The present volume has been conceived and richly illustrated as a publication to celebrate the reopening. It is dedicated not only to all the facets of its outstanding architecture, but also to aspects of the collection and the modernizations that were necessary to operate a modern museum. Our gratitude is extended not only to our publication department and the employees of the Neue Nationalgalerie, but also and especially to Constanze von Marlin for her meticulous management of the publication, Martin Reichert (David Chipperfield Architects) for diverse consultations, and the graphic designers Heimann + Schwantes for an elegant and even noble book design that is apposite to this building.

Michael Eissenhauer and Christina Haak
Director-General and Deputy Director-General
of the Staatliche Museen zu Berlin

Transparency, openness, and modernity—these terms come to mind when I think of the Neue Nationalgalerie in my hometown, Berlin. For many years this simple beauty of steel, glass, and granite was separated from us Berliners by construction fences. Now I am very pleased that we will be able to visit the Neue Nationalgalerie again. I share this joy with many of my colleagues at Siemens who have missed this important symbol of cosmopolitanism and innovation in our company's founding city.

All of us can hardly wait to enter this wonderful museum again. A place that after the period of waiting will now once again bring people from the whole world together and that will exhibit the most significant works. I personally think back to the Gerhard Richter exhibition *Panorama* just under ten years ago. His *4900 Farben* (4900 Colors) in particular impressed me at the time. This work of art, which consists of 196 square color plates, showed me how diversely different colors can be composed. Such nuances can only be experienced in architecture that does not oppress the art but leaves it as it is—in its essence.

Ludwig Mies van der Rohe achieved this interaction in the form of significant architecture. The result was a great gift to Berlin, to Germany, and to the world. The Neue Nationalgalerie provides enduring inspiration for the future. The energy of this place radiates widely and sheds light on nearly all spheres of life. Inspired by the Bauhaus, it brings together art, science, and business and thus also achieves our new future site: Siemensstadt^2. It, too, is being planned and built with passion—for a district of the city that permits residents, the company, and research to coexist without barriers.

Mies van der Rohe made it clear to us how much we need this form of openness. Architecture that opens up to people, in which inside and outside transition into each other. It makes possible new ideas and inventions that let people out into the world. From Berlin into the world.

Cedrik Neike
Member of the Board of Siemens AG

N A L G

NEUE NATIONALG

ERIE

50

Space and Structure

From the interior, the pavilion of the Neue Nationalgalerie (New National Gallery) frames the mural of the reborn city that has been growing around it. From outside, the reflections in the glass enclosure mirror those framed views. This shifting and superimposed reflectivity, which has become a subject prized by critics and photographers,[1] captures the phenomenal experience of the pavilion. Moving across the podium, the pedestrian is confronted by the glass wall recessed beneath the ponderous roof. Any anticipation of entering a closed inner sanctum gives way as one is drawn into the sheltering structure set apart from and above the city, poised on the hilltop, recalling Mies's description of the Museum for a Small City, where the "barrier between the artwork and the living community is erased" and the works become "elements in space against an open and ever-changing background."[2]

Since the late 1920s, Mies had envisioned the artistic and tectonic potential of glass and the steel skeleton frame in articulating space freely, opening it up, and connecting it to the landscape to fulfill the needs of humankind.[3] Structure and space, interior and exterior were, for him, indissoluble: "'It is neither core nor shell; it is all one.' The exterior and interior of my buildings are one. You cannot divorce them. The outside takes care of the inside."[4]

This is implicit in Seagram, where space projects back and forth across the landscaped plaza from the McKim, Mead and White building to the Picasso stage curtain, the glass box of Farnsworth with its embrace of the natural context, the interiority of Crown Hall as it opens to framed views of treetops, and overwhelmingly, under the weighty black roof of the Neue Nationalgalerie. Like a clearing in the forest, where a void is formed by the surrounding trees, Mies's pavilion invokes freedom, freedom of movement within a space that does not dictate. The shifting qualities of light that penetrate the space of the pavilion emit in equal measure mystery and tranquility: the ultimate expression of *beinahe Nichts.*

Phyllis Lambert

1 See, among others, Colin Rowe (with Robert Slutsky), "Transparency: Literal and Phenomenal," in Colin Rowe, *The Mathematics of the Ideal Villa and Other Essays* (Cambridge, MA: The MIT Press, 1976), pp 159–83; Robin Evans, "Mies van der Rohe's Paradoxical Symmetries," in *Translations from Drawings to Buildings and Other Essays* (Cambridge, MA: The MIT Press, 1997); Stan Allen, "Mies's Theatre of Effects, the New National Gallery, Berlin," in *Practice: Architecture, Technique, and Representation*, essays by Stan Allen, commentary by Diana Agrest (Amsterdam: G+B Arts International, 2000), pp. 71–85; Terence Riley and Barry Bergdoll, eds., *Mies in Berlin* (New York: MoMA and Abrams, 2001); and the portfolios of photographs commissioned for *Mies in America*.

2 MvdR, "Museum for a Small City"; Fritz Neumeyer, *The Artless Word: Mies van der Rohe on the Building Art*, trans. Mark Jarzombek (Cambridge, MA: The MIT Press, 1991), p. 322.

3 MvdR, "Was wäre Beton, was Stahl ohne Spiegelglas?"; Neumeyer, *The Artless Word*, p. 314.

4 MvdR, quoted in Katharine Kuh, "Mies van der Rohe: Modern Classicist," *Saturday Review* 48, no. 4 (January 23, 1965), pp. 22–23, esp. p. 22.

Originally published in Phyllis Lambert, ed., *Mies in America*, exh. cat. Canadian Centre for Architecture, Montreal, and Whitney Museum, New York (New York: Harry N. Abrams, 2001), p. 499.

GEMÄLDEGALERIE

The Temple

Transparency and Monumentality

Fritz Neumeyer

1.

It is unsurprising that most critics have viewed the Nationalgalerie in Berlin, since the time it was built, and its extravagant steel-and-glass pavilion on a stone podium quite naturally as a temple. This refers to the impressive image of a building with columns enthroned majestically on a substructure and hence recognizable even from afar as a public edifice. Even today, this memorable comparison shapes our perception of this Mies project, and rightly so, since classical and modern, monumentality and transparency, are combined in this building as in no other of the twentieth century.

Allusions to classical architecture were a matter of course for Ludwig Mies van der Rohe. That is evident already in his early work. Even just his penchant for always placing his buildings on a pedestal supports the impression of classical monumentality. Mies's very first building, the Riehl House in the Potsdam neighborhood of Neubabelsberg (fig. 1), already impressively reveals this disposition, namely, a prostyle placed asymmetrically—not to say picturesquely—on a podium. Shortly before that, in 1907, Peter Behrens had based his crematorium building in Hagen on this temple motif in strictly geometrical and symmetrical form. In 1908, Behrens again attracted attention with a building that recalled a temple, this time employing a steel-and-glass construction and an abstract form. The reference is to his famous turbine hall for AEG in the Moabit district of Berlin; a foundational building for modernism, which is not missing from any architectural history of the twentieth century. In 1909, the year the turbine hall was completed, Mies began working in Behrens's studio in Neubabelsberg.

The architectural design of the classical temple had long since emancipated itself from its original definition as a house of divinity and also from the building type of a windowless shrine surrounded by columns and hermetically sealed by walls. What survived was the memorable picture of a temple in an elevated location along with a form of architectural beauty, including the classical column placements and noble proportions. In the landscape garden of the eighteenth century, the temple was secularized once and for all. As an indispensably picturesque medium of atmosphere in classical scenery, it was built as a gabled temple, round temple, even sunken temple, or as a ruin. Also as a place of retreat for contemplation, from which the landscape could be experienced as an aesthetic spectacle, or conceived as a more or less sentimental sacred place; the Temple of Wisdom, Temple of Solitude, Temple of Love, and the like were intended to combine such philosophical or literary thinking with the landscape garden.

His architecture was also in a new light with regard to the original function of the classical temple. The classical temple is not only defined structurally by the enclosed space of the cella which lies in sacred darkness and is only accessible to the priest, but also by the contrasting open, publicly accessible in-between space of the ring of columns surrounding the cella outdoors. In his *Ästhetik* (published in English as *Aesthetics*), the Berlin philosopher Georg Friedrich Wilhelm Hegel gave his primary attention to this latter part of the classical temple and discovered it, so to speak, as the site of a self-determined public sphere where people come to themselves. Hegel writes:

> In these prostyles and amphiprostyles . . . , we see people wandering freely and openly, individually or in accidental groupings; for the colonnades as such enclose nothing but are the boundaries of open thoroughfares, so that people walking in them are half indoors and half outside and at least can always step directly into the open air. . . . Instead of having an idea of an assembly with a single aim, we see a drift outwards and get only the idea of people staying there cheerfully, without serious purpose, idly, and just chatting. . . . After all, the impression made by these temples is of simplicity and grandeur, but at the same time of cheerfulness, openness, and comfort, because the whole building is constructed for standing about in or strolling up and down in or coming and going rather than for assembling a collection of people and concentrating them there, shut in on every side and separated from the outside world.[1]

The significance of the podium, with the open space of its column ranges, made the temple Hegel's model for an architecture of coming and going; and if one thinks of Mies's temple when reading these lines, they anticipate the description of activities that could also play out at any time on the terrace of the Neue Nationalgalerie. But it is not necessary for the arc of thought to span that far, because already in Hegel's day, in the immediate vicinity of his apartment on the Kupfergraben, there was a comparable modern temple, which provided abundant space for such "standing about in or strolling up and down in or coming and going." From 1825 onward, Karl Friedrich Schinkel's Altes Museum (Old Museum) was built in the Lustgarten (Pleasure Garden) of Berlin (fig. 2). And one might think that Hegel had derived his view of the ancient temple from this Schinkel building—just as, conversely, Schinkel derived the idea for his building from Hegel's view of the temple.

Schinkel delimited the building in front with a colonnade and thus at the same time opened it up to the Lustgarten with a covered promenade. In it one finds oneself half inside, half outside, and can walk up and down the full length of the building. Receded behind this stoa is the open stairwell. Viewers walking on the latter become engaged in a visual dialogue with the space of the city (fig. 3). This stairwell offers a unique aesthetic experience of space. Around 1990, unfortunately, it fell victim to the later, temporary addition of a glass apron to provide a climate-controlled passageway. It has since become a permanent feature. On the upper stairwell, Schinkel transports viewers into a floating position halfway up the columns, one that can otherwise only be adopted on a scaffold. This floating observation—shifted into the building but still connected to the exterior—is a kind of belvedere on the threshold between interior and exterior. It is primarily intended for wandering around to revel in the view of the city and of oneself, and also to behold the works of art on the walls.

With this stairwell, Schinkel in principle anticipated the Miesian idea of the museum as a place where people encounter art and its surroundings. In his famous perspective view, Schinkel deliberately presented this space as one of curiosity and visual pleasure, of views in and out, of making contact and dreamily wandering about—and of course also as a place to encounter art. And so, as in Hegel, the temple does not become the focus of attention for its true purpose; the museum is not primarily seen here as an educational

1 Ludwig Mies van der Rohe, Riehl House, Potsdam-Neubabelsberg, view from the lower garden, ca. 1907

2 Karl Friedrich Schinkel, Altes Museum (Old Museum), Berlin, perspective view from the Lustgarten, prior to 1825

3 Karl Friedrich Schinkel, Altes Museum (Old Museum), Berlin, perspective view from the gallery to the Lustgarten, 1829

institution, but rather as a place of informal encounter, stimulation, and pleasure in seeing and as a site of dialogue.

Schinkel made the freedom of moving in space and encountering the panorama of the city a special component of the aesthetic experience of the museum. It was Mies who offered, with his temple of steel and glass, the proof in that regard of Schinkel's modern synthesis of the experience of space and the enjoyment of art.

2.

Mies felt indebted to Schinkel in building the Nationalgalerie in Berlin. That is unmistakably evident from the final sentence of his brief explanatory text on his design of 1963, which speaks of the intention to construct "a clear and rigorous building" that "I believe is in harmony with Berlin's Schinkelian tradition."[2]

With his design, Mies was moving closer to Schinkel and had no desire to make a secret of it. What exactly this "harmony" might be was something that everyone could decide for themselves. Mies offered no explanatory hint, perhaps because he did not wish to, but perhaps also because he did not consider it at all necessary. For an architect like him who was given an opportunity to build a museum in Berlin, it went without saying that he would think of Schinkel's museum at the Lustgarten. He was very familiar with that building. Already in his early years in Berlin, Mies had learned to admire Schinkel from his teacher Peter Behrens. Visiting the Schinkel buildings in Berlin and Potsdam on the weekend was part of the obligatory program of every employee in Behrens's studio around 1910, as Mies recalled.

In conversation with Graeme Shankland in 1959, Mies called the museum at the Lustgarten "a beautiful building": "you could learn everything in architecture from it—and I tried to do that."[3] What Mies, as an admirer of the formal logic of Schinkel's architecture, could "learn" from this museum is revealed by certain parallels between the two buildings despite their differences in formal idiom.

Schinkel reduced the entire building volume optically to the simple tectonic structure of a large table. Its four legs are formed by the large pillars at the building's outer corners. By means of shadow gaps, they are separated optically from the building mass and made evident as such in the first place. On these apparent pillars lies a large, continuous plate: a flat room terminated horizontally by an entablature and roof parapet, borne by a majestic colonnade. An open stairway leads up to the base on which the whole thing rests.

For the upper hall, Mies chose a construction that at first glance seems equally simple, except that the legs of the table on the pedestal are not at the corners of the square roof plate but arranged in pairs at the center of the sides. Whereas Schinkel had marked the load-bearing corner pillars as such only by means of gaps, the load-bearing structure of Mies's building is of course not just an image but appears before our eyes spatially in real form. Eight steel columns, deliberately moved to the furthest edge of the roof plate, heave the immense coffered ceiling measuring nearly 65 by 65 meters upward and cause it to float. This steel structure, which seems simple but is highly refined in its details and very ambitious in its manufacturing, serves as a roof plate spanning a space that, as a result of the receding of the glass façade, steps out of the interior and into the exterior as an ambulatory. In this way, walking around between the columns becomes a part of the spatial experience of the museum before even entering it.

In 1943, in his design for a Museum of Modern Art, later renamed Museum for a Small City, Mies experimented for the first time with the idea of a transparent museum (fig. 4). The building was conceived as a single, large space with glass on all sides. Articulated only by freestanding walls, the interior was intended to offer a maximum of flexibility and spatial freedom—for the work of art and for the visitor. Such an "open plan" permits, Mies wrote, the works of art to be "seen against the surrounding hills." Only a steel-frame construction could make the volume this transparent and permit "a building with only three basic elements—a floor slab, columns and a roof plate."[4]

Mies's steel-and-glass architecture of the large hall of the Nationalgalerie in Berlin was the logical continuation of this idea or a load-bearing structure reduced to the architectonic minimum and a generous space free of supports.

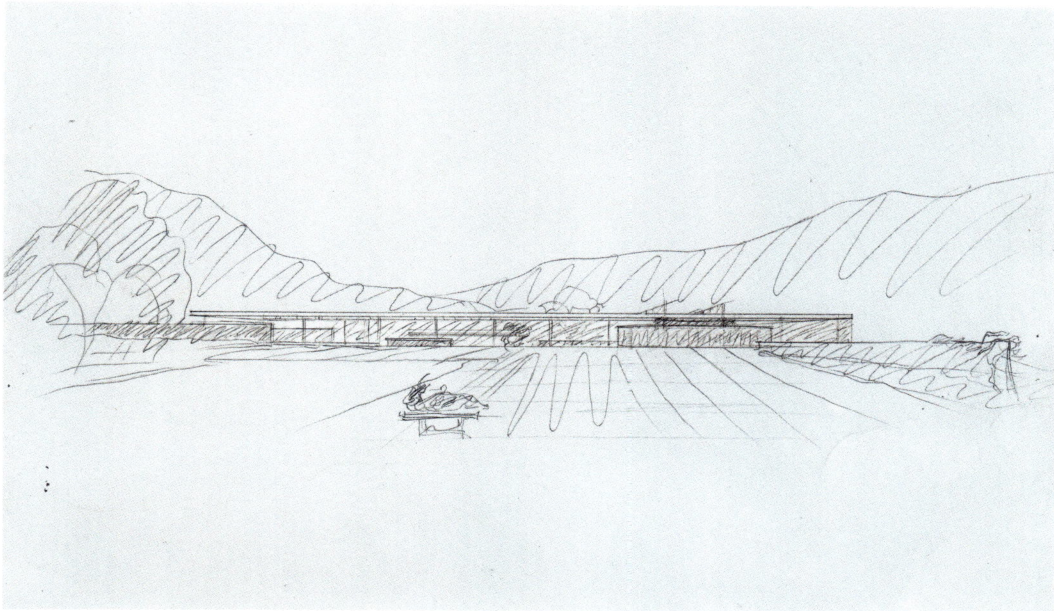

4 Ludwig Mies van der Rohe, Museum for a Small City, design, 1943

5 Karl Friedrich Schinkel, design for Orianda Palace, Crimea, 1838

6 Neue Nationalgalerie, northwest stairway to the podium, 1968

Only now did it become possible to realize in full Schinkel's suggestion of viewing works of art while wandering around freely against the backdrop of the panorama of the city and its bustle. Yet Schinkel may also have provided a crucial inspiration for the complete dissolution of the space-separating external wall into glass that Mies intended for his steel temple.

In Schinkel's idea design for Orianda Palace located on a plateau of a cliff above the Black Sea—a design with which Mies is known to have been very familiar—a temple that looms over the palace forms the highest point of the grounds (fig. 5). Schinkel imagined the intercolumniation of this temple in all glass, framed and supported by extremely thin metal frames. The fact that the lower building of this temple was also intended to house a large museum makes Schinkel's design an interesting parallel. It also included a *promenade architecturale* that led out of the lower building across grottos, vestibules, columned courtyards, and magnificent gardens up across a large stairway to the glass temple—a harbinger of the modern glass pavilion.

3.

Mies likewise transformed entering and walking through the museum into the impressive spatial experience of a *promenade architecturale*. It begins by ascending the open stairway to the granite-framed podium with a terrace that—elevated from ordinary street level—forms an urban plaza (fig. 6). In an urban-design wasteland with the presumptuous name Kulturforum, this is the only space that invites unplanned strolling and sitting in the open air. Entering beneath the vast coffered ceiling, the path leads past the slightly tapered steel columns that support it. One now finds oneself in a spatial layer that can already be perceived as an interior but belongs equally to the exterior. On entering the large hall, this perceptual logic is reversed, for now one finds oneself in an interior with the feeling of an exterior.

The fact that the exterior is omnipresent visually but acoustically excluded lends this space its unique atmosphere. Mies created something seemingly paradoxical: an interior that feels like an exterior. This room also derives its inner breadth from optically shifting the delimiting space on the sides beyond the terrace and the edge of the podium. The outer limit of this space is formed not by a wall but by the panorama of the city. The latter is placed immediately before the viewers' eyes but at the same time kept at a distance by the terrace of the podium on which the steel pavilion rests.

This grand interior imparts an exhilarating self-experience. The monumental coffered ceiling floating above our heads, its grid bearing the imprint of the coordinates of infinity, breathes a measure of generosity, expanse, freedom, solemnity, and determination that releases viewers from their world for a moment. Mies created a space for stepping aside in the very midst of the urban environment, a space that is oriented inward *and* outward at once (fig. 7), a space that invites contemplation but also reorganized attention. All of this together makes it a great, challenging space for the presentation of art.

Via freestanding stairs, the path leads out of the hall down into the basement, into a spacious, central, enclosed space. The entrances to the exhibition spaces are located in this foyer. They allow, for the most part, a flexible partitioning of space and have their spatial point of reference in the sculpture garden, which is accessible. As an interior in the exterior, the courtyard, which is open to the sky but closed on all sides, forms a kind of complementary endpoint of the entire spatial sequence. It describes an architectonically defined museum landscape that leads from the open expanse to the enclosed spatial form—and back. It offers a morphological sequence of art spaces of intrinsic value. It spans from the omnipresence of the public space in the interior to the intimate exhibition gallery and the quiet seclusion of a *hortus conclusus*.

4.

Mies reserved the freedom to distance himself from both modernist and traditional dogmas and conventions in equal measure. No other architect pursued with the same rigor the modern aesthetic of abstraction and reduction to the essentials and yet realized at the same time a monumental solemnity of form whose serenity and effect of the little and great radiates classical beauty and elegance.

Mies's buildings seem uncompromisingly modern and yet possess classical overtones at the same time. This impression already begins with the unusual combination of supposedly antithetical building materials, namely, industrially manufactured modern materials such as steel and glass or brick with selected, precious natural materials such as marble or onyx or travertine and wood. This combination alone makes it evident that an architectural artist was not willing simply to throw old values overboard in the name of the new, as most of his orthodox modern colleagues did—who, in the name of functionality and equality, regarded the Miesian repertoire of marble, travertine, raw-silk curtains, and so on, as the devil's work.

But the clarity of structure, the sense of proportions, and the architectonic relation of the parts to create a whole, as well as the flawlessness of the execution, also make Mies's buildings almost classical. As early as 1956, Ludwig Hilberseimer cited the Doric temple as a comparison in his book on Mies in order to explain the principles of Miesian architecture.[5]

Mies followed a philosophy of contrasts in which one legitimized the other. Monumentality obtains its right to exist only in dialogue with a complementary opposite: transparency and openness. The same is true in reverse. Only in the contrast does each experience its determination and significance as part of the whole. This dual orientation, which is intended to protect against one-sidedness, was expressed extremely clearly by Mies in 1924 in the final sentence of a lecture, worded as follows: "While we want to stand with both feet firmly on the ground, we want to reach with our head to the clouds."[6]

This attitude appeals in equal measure to earth and heaven, to material and spirit, as two poles of a fundamentally different orientation of human life. To persist positivistically solely in the existing and giving, and to seek one's salvation in materialism and in practical necessities and functional thinking, was just as one-sided and inadequate for Mies as the precise opposite, namely, losing one's grounding, circumventing the impositions of the given, and floating away into the realm of ideas and the absolute. Combining the sense for the near and real with the sense for the distant and ideal characterizes what Mies once called the double way into the immanent.[7] That way is cleared by the insight that we cannot take the one path without the other.

This form of worldview also determined Mies's architectural conviction of combining the real with the idea, the useful with the beautiful, the old with the modern. Probably more so than any other building, the Nationalgalerie Berlin turned that principle of 1924 concretely into architecture. With its stony pedestal growing out of the ground, the building stands with both legs firmly on the ground, unshakable, as if it were created for eternity; with its transparent steel pavilion, it raises its head into the clouds and realizes a dream of the freedom of movement in space in which the horizon and the panorama of the city appear before our eyes in the interior of a building.

5.

In 1905, the art critic Julius Meier-Graefe asked the question, with an eye to Peter Behrens, as to whether it would not be possible "to build in such a way that nothing of the form but only this cool spirit of the Greeks that is so worthy of adoration be resurrected?"[8] Sixty years later, Mies van der Rohe offered the appropriate architectonic response to this question with his building in Berlin. It is not only the final building by Mies whose completion and dedication he lived to see; it is also the apex, and at the same time the endpoint, of a development. Mies strove to derive from the rationality and sobriety of skeleton architecture an energy of form that could produce the feeling of classical physicality and even of the monumental, without burdening it with superfluous visual mass or formal components. In no other project did Mies get closer to his goal of transforming technology into the art of the building and elevating the technical construction of the steel skeleton to an architectural order of significance by means of reduction and refinement. That the steel

7 Neue Nationalgalerie, view of urban space from the exhibition hall, 1968

supports of the Nationalgalerie in Berlin are once again referred to in the plans as "columns" indicates that Mies believed that he could in fact achieve that here.

The example of columns gives us reason to suspect that Mies also wanted to see something comparable to a temple in this building. Mies was searching for and found classical form in the technical means themselves. And he stuck to it even when it could no longer be found in them. For in architecture, it is not technology but rather the architectonic sense that has the last word on form. That is why he had his steel supports taper slightly toward the top, an entasis of sorts that is characteristic of classical columns. This necessitated a considerable effort of extremely precise welding work. For these columns are not, as one might assume, four industrial steel T beams welded together to form a cross, but rather a form composed of individually customized steel plates welded together (fig. 8). The large coffered ceiling demanded an even more elaborate construction process. In order to make it appear to be horizontal and floating, its separate segments had to be calculated individually and be customized to a curve. With corresponding elevations, it prevents the roof plate from sagging in the middle and sinking at the corners.

As an architect, Mies was convinced that construction and technology, as the elementary facts of all building, also had to be the foundation of artistic expression in architecture. As an artist, therefore, Mies never abandoned the hope that modern steel construction could be conquered in the formal sense of architecture and be elevated aesthetically into an order with opportunities for spiritual expression—comparable to the architectural achievements of past eras and their building materials.

Mies took the industrially standardized steel T, double-T, and I beams found in nearly every building since the late nineteenth century beyond their technical form and transformed them into conveyors of meaning. No other architect was able to elevate this essentially banal constructional element to the rank of a defining component of true architecture, or to derive from its slimness the monumental dignity and noble elegance of classical form. For decades, Mies had refined his philosophy of the steel skeleton in Chicago. Its summa took on built form in Berlin: in a building in which the oscillation between classical temple and the technology of the industrial age is present—in opposites that enter into a dialogue with each other.

1 Friedrich Wilhelm Hegel, *Aesthetics* (1830), trans. T. M. Knox, 2 vols. (1966), pp. 2: 675–76.
2 Ludwig Mies van der Rohe, *Berlin: Galerie des 20. Jahrhunderts*, presentation portfolio for the Neue Nationalgalerie building of 1963, fol. 1, Kunstbibliothek Berlin.
3 Mies van der Rohe interviewed by Graeme Shankland for the BBC Third Programme (1959), reprinted in Peter Carter, *Mies van der Rohe at Work* (London: Phaidon Press, 1999), pp. 180–82, esp. p. 182.
4 Ludwig Mies van der Rohe, "Museum for a Small City," *Architectural Forum* 78, no. 5 (May 1943), pp. 84–85. Reprinted in Fritz Neumeyer, *The Artless Word: Mies van der Rohe on the Building Art*, trans. Mark Jarzombek (Cambridge, MA: The MIT Press, 1991), p. 322.
5 Ludwig Hilberseimer, *Mies van der Rohe* (Chicago: Paul Theobald and Company, 1956), pp. 38–39.
6 Ludwig Mies van der Rohe, lecture manuscript of June 19, 1924, in Neumeyer, *The Artless Word*, pp. 249–50, esp. p. 250.
7 Ludwig Mies van der Rohe, "Notebook, 1927–1928," in Neumeyer, *The Artless Word*, pp. 265–96, esp. p. 283.
8 Julius Meier-Graefe, "Peter Behrens: Düsseldorf," *Dekorative Kunst* 8 (July 1905), pp. 381–428, esp. p. 389.

8 Neue Nationalgalerie, detail of column

Potsdamer Brücke (Potsdam Bridge) with the ruin of the Haus des Fremdenverkehrs (House of Tourism) at the corner of the street Reichpietschufer, Berlin, 1952

VOLKSWOHL
BUND

Neue Nationalgalerie under construction, May 1966

The building art is man's spatial dialogue with his environment and demonstrates how he asserts himself therein and how he masters it. For this reason, the building art is not merely a technical problem nor a problem of organization or economy.

The building art is in reality always the spatial execution of spiritual decisions. It is bound to its times and manifests itself only in addressing vital tasks with the means of its times. A knowledge of the times, its tasks, and its means is the necessary precondition of work in the building art.

Ludwig Mies van der Rohe, "The Preconditions of Architectural Work," 1928

Cornerstone ceremony of the Neue Nationalgalerie, September 23, 1965

Lower floor of the Neue Nationalgalerie under construction, October 1966

Raising of the roof of the Neue Nationalgalerie, April 5, 1967

Raising of the roof of the Neue Nationalgalerie, April 5, 1967

Ludwig Mies van der Rohe at the topping-out ceremony of the Neue Nationalgalerie, April 12, 1967

The glass skin, the glass walls alone permit the skeleton structure its unambiguous constructive appearance and secure its architectonic possibilities. . . .

They are genuine building elements and the instruments of a new building art. They permit a measure of freedom in spatial composition that we will not relinquish any more. Only now can we articulate space freely, open it up and connect it to the landscape. Now it becomes clear again what a wall is, what an opening, what is floor and what ceiling.

Ludwig Mies van der Rohe, "What Would Concrete, What Would Steel Be without Mirror Glass?," 1933

Ludwig Mies van der Rohe's speech at the topping-out ceremony of the Neue Nationalgalerie, April 12, 1967

Topping-out wreath in the form of the exhibition hall of the Neue Nationalgalerie, 1967

Construction site of the Neue Nationalgalerie, 1967

Fußgänger
bitte andere
Gehwegseite
benutzen

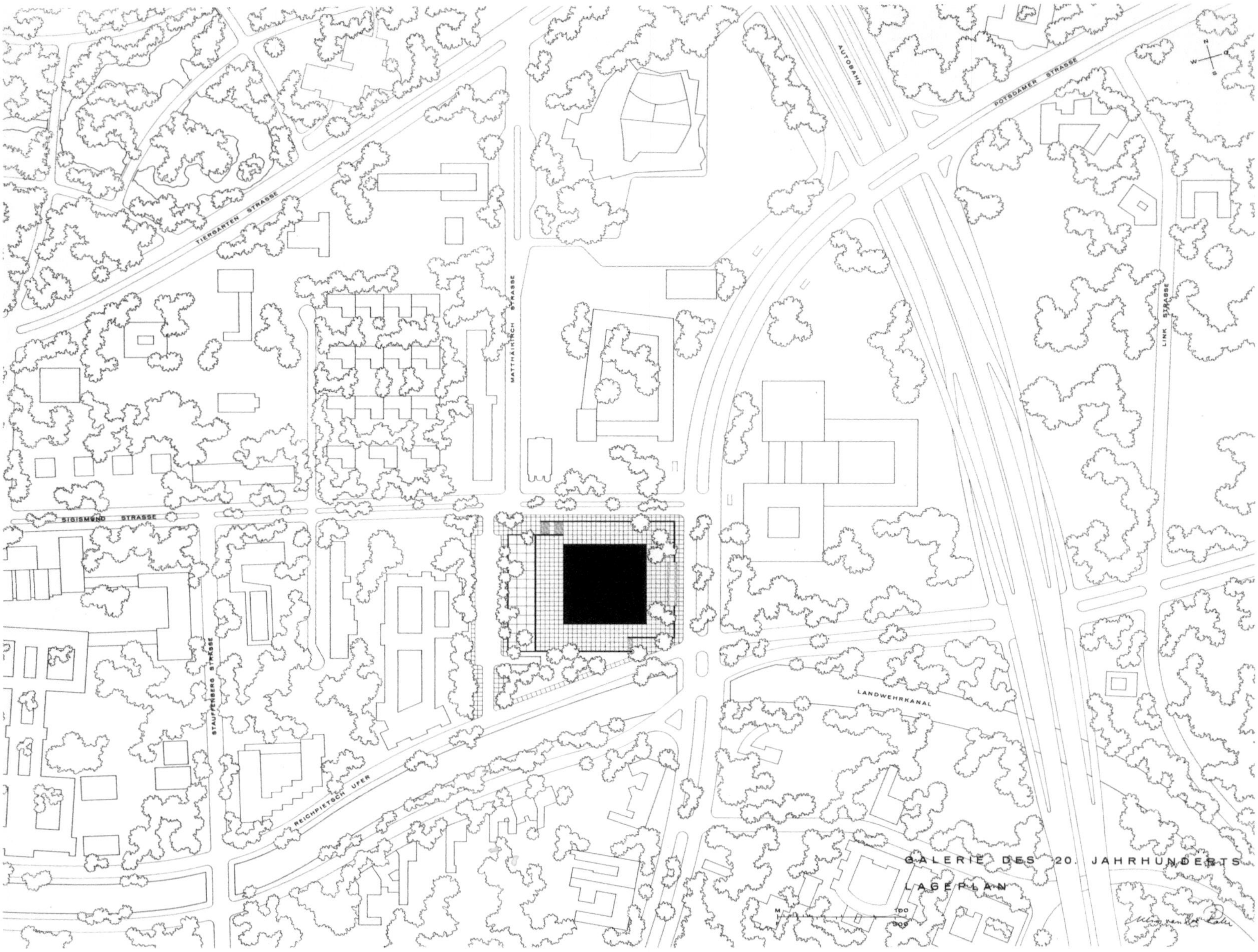

Ludwig Mies van der Rohe, site plan from the presentation portfolio for the Neue Nationalgalerie, 1963

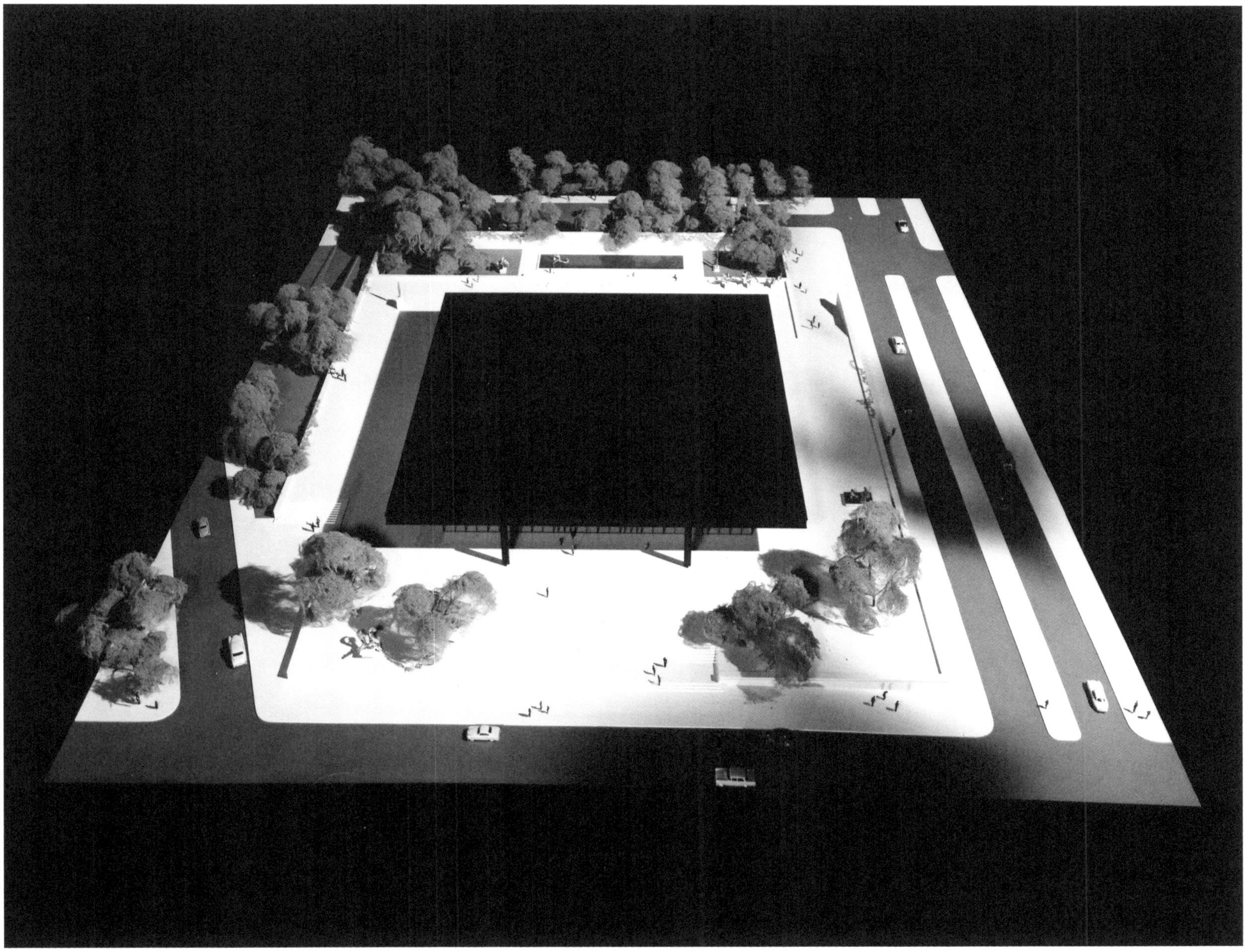

Ludwig Mies van der Rohe, photo of model from the presentation portfolio for the Neue Nationalgalerie, 1963

The Backstory

Dirk Lohan

As a young architect in the 1960s, I worked in the office of my grandfather Ludwig Mies van der Rohe in Chicago. I was there from the start when the idea of granting him an architectural commission evolved into a real project in West Berlin. My memories are still vivid, because they were the first and most valuable experiences of my professional life.

There were several attempts after the Second World War to commission Mies van der Rohe to work in Berlin. He was invited to participate in the *Internationale Bauausstellung* (International Architecture Exhibition) in 1957 in the Hansaviertel (Hansa District). He was sent a 30-centimeter-high stack of building codes and rules for the architecture of social housing. He responded that he would like to build a residential high-rise in Berlin, specifically one of steel and glass similar to the 860–880 Lake Shore Drive Apartments in Chicago (fig. 3). That did not work, of course, because Interbau was intended to present solutions to social housing financed with public funds. A high-rise of steel and glass of the sort that Mies was the first to build in Chicago would have been too expensive for the situation in West Berlin two decades after the Second World War. So Mies was one of the most prominent absentees at Interbau.

In the later 1950s, on the occasion of his second or third visit to Germany—he still hadn't been back to Berlin—Senate Building Director Werner Düttmann sought him out in Aachen, and the two men spoke of a possible architecture project for a gallery of the twentieth century. This idea evolved into a real project, and in 1962 Mies was commissioned to design it. He was suffering from severe arthritis at that time and could neither stand nor walk, so that a complicated operation on his hip joint became necessary. He was in the hospital for weeks and then stayed at home for months thereafter. The first design ideas were worked out by his long-standing employee Gene R. Summers, who imagined a two-story building with a rectangular floor plan and steel supports over the roof like those of Crown Hall in Chicago, but with the ground floor receded (fig. 1). The office produced beautiful drawings and a large model of this idea. Summers set this model up in Mies's room at the hospital in order to get his opinion. After a long silence, Mies said: "Forget it, we are going to do the Bacardi/Schäfer concept. That belongs to Berlin."

1 Ludwig Mies van der Rohe, Crown Hall, campus of the Illinois Institute of Technology, Chicago, Illinois, 1956

2 Ludwig Mies van der Rohe, architectural model for the Ron Bacardi headquarters in Cuba, 1958

3 Ludwig Mies van der Rohe, 860–880 Lake Shore Drive Apartments, Chicago, ca. 1960

4 Exhibition architecture for the opening exhibition by Mies van der Rohe's office, 1968

The idea of an enormous square slab supported by eight columns, two on each side, had preoccupied him for years. He first developed the idea for a project in Cuba (fig. 2). This temple of concrete for the rum producer Bacardi was never built, because Fidel Castro's rise to head of government and president put an end to it. The design was further developed for a version in steel for the painting collection of Georg Schäfer in Schweinfurt. As the building plans for Berlin took concrete form, the collection generously released this project from its contract. Mies knew what he wanted and often said that this concept paid homage to Karl Friedrich Schinkel and that Schweinfurt was not the right place for it. In Berlin, there was no proper client. The building was commissioned by the Berlin Senate. The space allocation program was devised in a number of all-night conversations between Senate Building Director Werner Düttmann and Mies in Berlin and Chicago. At the time, Berlin did not own nearly enough paintings for the walls of such a museum. Nevertheless, Düttmann and the Senator for Building, Rolf Schwedler, aggressively pushed the gigantic undertaking. The relationship between the main protagonists was decidedly affectionate, and after several boozy and merry evenings they were on a first-name basis. They laughed a lot and joked with typical Berliner wit—Düttmann was a master at that.

From the outset, I was working for the Neue Nationalgalerie, initially under the direction of Summers. After he left the firm, I took over responsibility for the project. It was a wonderful task for me to work together with my grandfather on an important building. The Nationalgalerie was doubtless the final building project in which Mies was very personally interested. Over the years of its planning and building, we spent countless hours together discussing the details, sketching, and also rejecting many things that had become part of the standard fittings in other projects. For example, it was his idea not to have the cover of the large hall concealed by a suspended plaster ceiling under it. He believed that the hall should be used like a stage where exhibitions are dramatized, each different from the last, always refreshing and surprising in its presentation of art (fig. 4).

During the planning, Mies expressed the desire to see a large model of the supporting plate to be able to determine whether the roof truly looked flat. He was always very concerned about studying optical refinements by using mock-ups that were as large as possible. So we built a full view of the hall at a scale of 1:5 on one long wall of the office. Mies sat in front of it in his wheelchair, screwed up his eyes, and studied the subtlest shifts for hours. All of us found it extremely interesting to discover that the four corners of the roof plate created the visual impression that they hung downward. It took raising them by 5 centimeters and elevating the center of the roof by 10 centimeters to produce the desired impression of a freely floating, truly flat roof.

Another refinement of its architectonic appearance, compared to the designs for Bacardi and Schäfer, was the tapering of the eight columns. These supports were steel plates welded together, and it would have been normal to have these plates running in parallel at the same width across the entire height. Mies proposed instead that we should study whether a tapering of the columns upward would produce a more convincing look, similar to the entasis of the famous stone columns of the Parthenon on the Acropolis in Athens. We then drew various versions of columns with very different dimensions and produced a few models of columns at the scale of the building model. These variations were also evaluated for a long time by all of us, until one day Mies pointed to the solution that was then used for the building. To my knowledge, it is decidedly rare for modern architects to study such visual refinements. That was an interesting experiment for the younger team members on this project.

One day, we were visited by around fifteen Russian architects from Moscow, for whom meeting the master, who was famous in the Soviet Union as well, was a great event. I gave them a tour and explained our works. Among other things, I showed them a beautiful model of the Neue Nationalgalerie that the workshop had just finished. For this model, we had made very small but pretty Barcelona tables and chairs of glass, leather, and steel, which were waiting to be inserted into the model. After the Russians had left the workshop, a young employee ran after us and, aghast, reported that half of the furnishings had disappeared. There was, of course, only one suspicion. We quickly headed to the lobby of the office to demand the return of our Barcelona chairs. Ashamed and with averted eyes, the Russian architects removed their trophies from their pockets, and we were able to complete our model for Berlin. Yes, the dream to own a Barcelona chair had penetrated even the Iron Curtain.

The museum had long been under construction when the idea came up to give the building to the Stiftung Preussischer Kulturbesitz (Prussian Cultural Heritage Foundation). So we had a client after all and now feared there would be big changes. Fortunately, that was not the case; our relationships with the director general of the Staatliche Museen zu Berlin (National Museums in Berlin), Stephan Waetzoldt, and the founding director of the museum, Werner Haftmann, were decidedly good. When Haftmann had just been appointed, Mies invited him to his suite at the Hilton Hotel and prepared me: "Tonight, we will drink a good wine with him, then we will get to know him." Haftmann's reputation for greatly appreciating a good red wine preceded him. I remember only that the evening ran very long and that I could not keep up with the two elderly gentlemen. In any case, Haftmann ordered the best French wines several times, because my choice did not entirely please him. The bill was correspondingly high, but the friendship was sealed!

So the space allocation program was retained. Beneath the large hall, in the basement of the building, are the rooms for the permanent collection of the Neue Nationalgalerie. They open to the west into the equally expansive museum garden. Whereas the exhibition hall represents the architectural attraction, the more or less conventional accommodations for the permanent collection are just as important for the presentation of works of art of extraordinarily high quality.

The first exhibition in the new building was dedicated to the Dutch painter Piet Mondrian. Director Haftmann felt that Mondrian was particularly well suited to Mies van der Rohe. Mies was not at all pleased by it, because he knew very well how small most Mondrian paintings are. He was aware that, despite their brilliance, these small works would not be able to fill out the large hall. So I decided on a system of hanging walls that had the visual mass to scale the space into sections. The Mondrians were to be hung on these floating

5 Director Werner Haftmann during the hanging of the *Piet Mondrian* exhibition, 1968

6 Raising of the roof of the Neue Nationalgalerie, April 5, 1967

walls. Prior to the opening in September 1968, the paintings were brought into the hall, and the curators, under Haftmann's direction, began to hang them (fig. 5). When I joined them, I saw that the paintings had been attached at a slightly downward slope from the walls. When I asked why, I was told that the glass walls of the hall reflected in the glazed paintings, and that was unacceptable. After much back and forth, I insisted that the paintings be hung vertically, as otherwise they would have disturbed the whole architectural quality of the hall. Naturally, I had discussed it by phone with Mies in Chicago, who at the advanced age of eighty-two was too weak to come to the opening. The discussion between Werner Haftmann and me grew so heated that we could not ultimately arrive at an agreement, and he took the rest of the day off. I have asked myself many times since how many of the participants in the opening celebrations looked at the paintings at all. It was, after all, primarily an architectural event.

Mies's final visit to Berlin was for the raising of the enormous roof in April 1967. The entire steel roof had been welded together on the terrace, and the plan was to erect it completely in just one day. The steel construction company responsible, Krupp-Druckenmüller, was very pleased that the Deutscher Betontag (German Concrete Day) was to be held in the neighboring Philharmonie (Philharmonic Hall) that same day. One cannot have wished for a more convincing demonstration of the advantages of steel on that day: in the morning, when the Betontag delegates entered the Philharmonie, the large steel plate was lying on the ground; at the end of the day, when they went home, the temple was standing there. It had been raised by the so-called lift slab construction method, in which the roof is pulled up step by step (fig. 6). The lifting process took around eight hours. When the roof was 2 meters above the ground, Mies absolutely wanted to walk under it to see whether the nascent space lived up to his idea. Accompanied by me, he walked laboriously on two crutches under the floating roof. As Mies admired the majestic size of the roof, I was primarily concerned with standing under one of the open fields in case the gigantic steel plate should come crashing down. Mies, by contrast, walked around below it as if the building were already finished. I had the impression that being buried under this plate would have seemed to him to be a worthy fate. Mies was distinctly unsentimental, and his memories always brought laughs. For example, looking back to the closing of the Bauhaus, he would recall very comic situations. He had learned that sentimentality and nostalgia were feelings that didn't help him. So it was only on his third visit to Berlin, on the occasion of the museum's cornerstone ceremony in 1965, that he sought out, at my suggestion, the places of his earlier life. On one weekend, we traveled to the AEG production plant, visited the old factory that had housed the Bauhaus, and saw the Perls House. He told me a lot about his time with Peter Behrens and surprised me with measurements down to the millimeter of the AEG turbine hall—and that from someone who could not precisely remember the dimensions of the grid of the Neue Nationalgalerie. Today, fifty years later, I can understand that well, because I too can still remember only the numbers of my first important building: those of the Neue Nationalgalerie.

After the Neue Nationalgalerie opened, the upper hall was repeatedly criticized: it was unsuitable for many art exhibitions, above all because the façade is all glass, and the interior is very tall and constructed without fixed walls. This criticism has come primarily from museum directors and curators, since most museums have rooms and walls in which exhibitions can be hung without making big changes. Interestingly, however, over the course of the years it has turned out that this criticism was unjustified, because, as the present volume convincingly demonstrates, curators and artists have designed wonderful exhibitions that presented art as never before. One can say that art really has to be shown in this building as if on a stage—just as Mies had intended. He owned a considerable art collection himself, and his goal was to produce a universal space in which any art—from small to large format or even an installation—is at home. I'm convinced that he would have been thrilled if he could have seen the exhibitions of the past fifty years.

Neue Nationalgalerie shortly before the opening, 1968

I hope to make my buildings neutral frames in which man and artworks can carry on their own lives.

Ludwig Mies van der Rohe in conversation with
Christian Norberg-Schulz, 1958

Opening ceremony of the Neue Nationalgalerie, September 15, 1968

Opening exhibition, *Piet Mondrian*, 1968

Opening ceremony of the Neue Nationalgalerie, September 15, 1968

Sculpture garden of the Neue Nationalgalerie, 1968

Terrace with the sculpture *The Archer*, 1964–65, by Henry Moore, 1968

Terrace with the sculpture *Têtes et Queue* (Heads and Tail), 1965, by Alexander Calder, 1968

The glass exhibition hall and collection floor of the Neue Nationalgalerie at night, 1968

FEUERSOZIETAT

Kenneth Snelson exhibition, 1977

François Morellet exhibition, 1977

François Morellet exhibition, 1977

The Museum

The Neue Nationalgalerie in Mies van der Rohe's Oeuvre

Wolf Tegethoff

Mies is building in Berlin![1]—in 1963, the Senate of West Berlin entrusted Ludwig Mies van der Rohe with his most elaborate building project yet: the new museum building not yet known as the Nationalgalerie but rather conceived as the municipal exhibition venue and gallery of the twentieth century in the southern part of the Tiergarten district (fig. 1).[2] Initially, almost without exception, the response to this news from the press and the public was positive, indeed almost enthusiastic. After several failed attempts, one had finally succeeded in connecting the man whom many saw as the most important representative of contemporary architecture back to his former sphere of activity, after having emigrated to Chicago twenty-five years earlier, by commissioning a building in Germany. The exodus of the old avant-garde driven by National Socialism had left behind a vacuum in Berlin especially, with consequences that could still be felt everywhere, even two decades after the war had ended. Increasingly aware of their own provincialism, one was ultimately searching for the connection to exiled modernism, which—very much in the tenor of the time—was often covered up as a "belated act of making amends."

The appointment of Mies van der Rohe should be seen against that backdrop. It is, in any case, the only way to explain the unusual number of concessions granted by the client, which in the preliminary negotiations in 1961 had even left the choice of architectural brief to the architect's preference.[3] The reproach often expressed later—that the Nationalgalerie building dominates the works of art shown there by subordinating them to its own artistic ambition—thus ignores the real intentions and objectives of the decision-makers at the time: the most urgent concern of the Berlin Senate when commissioning the building was not to create space to house a collection of paintings that was still just being assembled at the time; the focus of interest—sources leave little doubt about this—was in fact clearly the desire for an epochal document of modern architecture in Berlin, and Mies van der Rohe's age and the state of his health called for urgency.

The problematic aspects of the design presented in the spring of 1963 and then exhibited publicly, which still influence some of the reservations of museum professionals about the Nationalgalerie building and thanks to stereotypical repetition still today continue to prevent serious engagement with the concept on which it is based, were by no means overlooked but clearly seen from the beginning.[4] All in all, however, it tended to be merely objections half-heartedly asserted that were easily able to undermine the sacrosanct authority of the likes of Mies van der Rohe by carping about function. Nevertheless, the indisputable conflict between the aesthetic ambition immanent in the architecture and the everyday demands of using a museum building, as evident in the Neue Nationalgalerie, is by no means purely formal in nature but rather the consequence of different views of fundamental questions related to the presentation and reception of art in the current context. The reproach of functional unsuitability presupposes a generally shared notion of the meaning and task of the museum as such. It further implies a clearly outlined program based on that, which provides a solid framework for the architecture and hence can establish the sole standard for an appropriate judgment. Setting aside the fact that, apart from specifying the floor area needed, the guidelines given to Mies van der Rohe were extremely vague and he was actually granted a great deal of freedom in the design,[5] the question remains: To what extent is such a concrete and generally applicable definition even possible today?

Stephan Waetzoldt had clearly identified the dilemma already in 1971 with regard to the planned additional new museum buildings on Kemperplatz:

> The museum today can no longer present itself as clearly [as it still could in the nineteenth century]. That is not just because the task of the institution in respect to today's society of achievement and of the masses is anything but defined, but also because of a process of differentiation and specialization . . . . It is therefore equally nonsensical to speak of "the" museum or of museum architecture per se and in general. Museums are individuals with specific characteristics and a life history that is often long. They need—unfortunately—not off-the-rack but made-to-measure architecture.
> But where is one to find the measurements? Measurements and standards for museum architecture are set, first of all, by a number of given—objective—constants: the holdings and mission of the collection, the

1 View of the construction site of the Neue Nationalgalerie, 1966

2 Ludwig Mies van der Rohe, Resor House, perspective from the living room through the south façade, collage, 1937–41

3 Ludwig Mies van der Rohe, Museum for a Small City project, perspective of the interior, collage, 1942

> conditions set by conservation and exhibition technology, the urban-design situation, and the user structure . . . . Measurements and standards for museum architecture are also determined—in a crucial way—by variables that presume subjective analysis and interpretation of the future. . . . The goal is to give an institution an architectural form in which, as Klaus von Dohnanyi expressed it, the "third dimension" in education occurs: the awakening and developing of the creative imagination, grappling with aesthetic and historical qualities, encountering foreign and other ways of life. The museum can thus make a crucial contribution to the rational determination of one's own individual standpoint in today's world. For in contrast to all other educational institutions, which are oriented around defined learning goals, the museum is open. It makes encounter and discussion possible but does not force them. It can, if handled properly, be the democratic educational institution par excellence. . . . As a building for the public, however, the museum has to satisfy the natural and justified expectations of the population, which cannot be satisfied with the paltry functional building, the "art shed."[6]

In view of this complex initial situation, the criticism expressed seems trite and indiscriminating, because it has recourse one-sidedly to technical, functional deficits without considering their own relative value in the overall context of the task set. In the eyes of many museum professionals, the "paltry functional building," the "art shed," to use Waetzoldt's words, still represent a perfect framework for bringing out optimally the works of art preserved there. Architecture in the sense of the art of building, as it must be, should accordingly be limited to the outer shell and entrances areas not of further use for exhibition purposes, where it can at best serve to create a solemn mood for the experience of art waiting inside. In this polemic exaggeration of a nevertheless widespread basic attitude, the standards of value of a long-past nineteenth century emerge, yet they are hardly equal any longer to the changed expectations of a modern mass society. In their ultimate consequence, they aim for the total isolation of the work of art that, undisturbed by any foreign influences, can unfold whatever effect it might have in its lonely encounter with the viewer. Can this still succeed today? Could it ever succeed? And, last but not least: Can architecture ever satisfy such a demand without simultaneously calling into question any claim it might have to an autonomous creative power? Waetzoldt's reflections of 1971 were surely stimulated by discussions of the Neue Nationalgalerie, which was built during his term as director general of the Stiftung Preussischer Kulturbesitz (Prussian Cultural Heritage Foundation),[7] ultimately assigning to the architect the critical task of lending concrete form to his or her definition, in principle and in general, of a contemporary museum.

It is therefore time to inquire into the more profound intentions and goals that Mies himself associated with his design of the Neue Nationalgalerie. Other than a not very informative welcome address on the occasion of the opening on September 15, 1968, more detailed discussions of the building have not survived. As a basis for further study, we will therefore examine Mies van der Rohe's own ideas about the architectural presentation of works of art, the steps of which can be traced through his entire oeuvre.

With the final failure of the commission to build the Villa Kröller-Müller near The Hague in 1912, which led to a rift with his teacher Peter Behrens, Mies found himself, already at the very beginning of his career, confronted with the task of finding an appropriate way to present a considerable art collection to its advantage in a private home. Hermann Lange, whose home, built from 1927 to 1930, now houses temporary exhibitions of contemporary art of the Kunstmuseen Krefeld (Krefeld Art Museums), was another enthusiastic art lover and collector, which was also true of Eduard Fuchs and Erich Wolf, for whom Mies designed gallery additions in Berlin and Guben (now Gubin), respectively, in the late 1920s and early 1930s. The project of a house for Emil Nolde in the Zehlendorf district of Berlin, at the time of the Barcelona Pavilion of 1929, was intended to include both a studio and a larger exhibition hall for the artist's paintings but never went beyond the planning stage.[8] The architectural presentation of works of art thus played a key role in the oeuvre of Mies van der Rohe, and that was increasingly true from the 1930s onward. At the time, he began to experiment with walled-in garden courtyards that formed extension zones of the interior. The collages he made in the wake of these "courtyard house projects" were for the most part works produced by students in Chicago under Mies van der Rohe's supervision after his emigration but employing older sketches; they nevertheless represent his original intentions. The color reproductions used here of works by Georges Braque and Paul Klee, often just details, represent wall-sized, unframed paintings that articulate and provide accents in the open spatial structure in the interior of the buildings.

Similar collages can be found among the designs for the Resor House of 1937–38. The view of the living room reproduced here dates from circa 1940, so it was made only after the project had fallen through once and for all (fig. 2). For the first time, it features a painting confronted directly with a view into the landscape opening up beyond the all-glass outer wall. The effect of the resulting spatial impression is astonishing: whereas the luminous colors of Paul Klee's painting *Bunte Mahlzeit* (Colorful Meal, 1937) stand out starkly against the dark background and develop a remarkable effect showing the depth of the pictorial space, the framed view of the landscape behind it flattens into a pure prospect. The unframed, wall-sized painting determines to a large degree the spatial disposition of the living hall, which it at the same times shields from the outside, while the optically distorted view out seems like an inadequate, two-dimensional stage set. To the same degree that the landscape appears alienated and made unreal as a result, the work of art becomes an integral component of the immediate surroundings of the occupants.[9]

In February 1943, in the middle of the Second World War, when public and private construction activity had come nearly completely to a halt in America as well, the editors of *Architectural Forum* announced an idea competition with twenty-two invited architects.[10] They sought solutions for "non residential postwar buildings," to be published in the May issue of the journal.[11] Mies, who had been approached for an essay on church building, dedicated himself instead to the design of a Museum of Modern Art,[12] which was ultimately published under the name Museum for a Small City. The explanatory report he sent off in April provides insight into the architect's conceptual ideas, and their fundamental formulations still possess validity for the Nationalgalerie in Berlin:

> The first problem is to establish the museum as a center for the enjoyment, not the interrment [*sic*] of art. In this project the barrier between the art work and the living community is erased by a garden approach which displays sculpture. The interior sculptures enjoy an equal spatial freedom, because the open plan permits them to be seen against the surrounding hills. And what could be a more appropriate setting for sculpture than the landscape? The architectural space, thus achieved, becomes a defining rather than a confining space, and the effect of the room as a container is destroyed. A work such as Picasso's *Guernica* has been difficult to place in the usual museum gallery. Here it could be placed to greatest advantage and become an element in space as is the sculpture which affords views from all sides with equal advantage plus the variety of a changing background. The building, conceived as one large space, allows every flexibility in use. . . . Small pictures would be exhibited on free standing walls. The entire building is available for larger groups, encouraging a more representative use of the museum than is customary today, and creating a noble background for the civic and cultural life of the community.[13]

In the generally accepted view of the nineteenth century, the museum was seen primarily as an educational institution. As the treasury of the artistic legacy of past epochs and cultures and even of one's own nation, it presented to the outside the picture of an ideal world, strictly separated from everyday life and without any immediate connection to reality. Spatially isolated and secluded from the outside world by columned façades, stately foyers, and monumental stairways, it thus inevitably also prevented any unprejudiced and immediate access to the work of art itself. As a "temple of art," it lent a sacred solemnity to the treasures preserved there. It encouraged reverence of the great artistic achievements of the past, but not the living communication between work and viewers. The latter was, however, precisely the point from which Mies van der Rohe set out, radically breaking with traditional ideas. For him,

4 Ludwig Mies van der Rohe, Neue Nationalgalerie, design of the collection rooms, collage, 1963

5 View from the garden to the exhibition and collection floors of the Neue Nationalgalerie, 1968

the temples of art had transformed into mausoleums, into charnels for the relics of bygone eras. Rather than bringing them closer to the viewers, to simulate their enjoyment of works of art and thereby awaken them to new life, it had merely created more barriers. Mies therefore wagered everything on tearing down the barriers erected between work and viewers. The venerable shrine of the temple that he disparagingly described as a "container" had to be broken up and replaced by an open spatial structure in order to achieve once again living contact between the museum and the outside world. Therefore, when Mies spoke of paintings or sculptures first and foremost as spatial elements that want to be seen against the changing background of the surrounding landscape, he was appealing to the totalizing way of seeing of the material world, and the goal was to restore that. Painting and sculpture had a crucial role in this, as should be shown using the example of the Resor House collage: the breaking up of the container—which is now no longer a spatial cell forced between walls closed on all sides—already resulted in a completely new experience of space. Moreover, this space had to remain identifiable as a protected area within the open landscape. Or, paraphrasing Mies again, a building that is no longer firmly delimited and thereby closed off from the soundings nevertheless requires a certain spatial definition, which ensures its autonomy despite all the emphatic openness. Paintings and sculpture, which are comparable in their function to the freestanding walls in Mies van der Rohe's buildings of the 1920s, thereby represent the decisive spatial fixed points. Mies countered the traditionally introverted architecture of the nineteenth century emphasizing spatial separation with an extroverted alternative.

A collage from the Museum for a Small City project may help to explain this further using the example of a specific case (fig. 3). It features no perspective lines but still conveys a spatial impression that is convincing at first glance—ignoring the fact that the interior depicted here contradicts all of our visual experiences and could never exist in this form. The upper edge and lower edge of the two full-height openings in the walls run along different horizontal levels that cannot be extended into any uniform floor or ceiling plane. The suggested spatial impression is thus inherently inconsistent. The spatial effect of the collage with which Mies already crosses the line between architectural rendering and autonomous work of art is based entirely on the parallel arrangement of the planes of the overlapping elements of "views into the open," "sculptures," and "paintings."

With an addition to the Museum of Fine Arts in Houston, the Cullinan Wing of 1954–58, Mies was given the opportunity for the first time to put into practice his ideas of the meaning and task of a museum. The immediate precursor of the Neue Nationalgalerie was not Houston, however, but rather the project for the Museum Georg Schäfer in Schweinfurt (1960–62). Its basic concept—albeit with considerably enlarged structural volumes—could be adopted, only slightly transformed, for Berlin.[14] The design for Schweinfurt already featured a glass hall, symmetrical on all sides, with a broadly projecting roof and two cruciform columns moved inward from the sides above a subterranean floor extended into a podium, though still without the sunken sculpture courtyard. Nearly all of these elements were found in similar form in the also unrealized headquarters of the Ron Bacardi Company (fig. 2, p. 58) for Santiago de Cuba (1957–60), whereby the prototype—a square glass hall with supports flanged in the center of the sides above a gridded platform—was already established in the ideal design of the Fifty by Fifty Feet House of 1950–52 (fig. 1, p. 163). The close relationship of these projects so different in their brief (residence, headquarters, museums)—which Mies himself never tried to keep secret, by the way—provided critics of the Nationalgalerie with confirmation of their criticism that it was functionally unsuitable as a museum. The objective of this criticism overlooks the further-reaching intentions of the architect, whose entire effort was to restore a totalizing image of the world—and he was surely aware that his goal could at best be achieved only on a purely aesthetic level. The goal of his efforts as an architect was not additional separation but rather the integration of spheres of life that were drifting apart. This guiding idea is expressed for the first time in a brief quotation about the Farnsworth House (1945–51), but it can easily be applied to the later museum projects: "But we should try to bring nature, buildings and human beings together in a higher unity. When you see nature through the glass walls of the Farnsworth house it takes on a deeper meaning . . . . More is asked for from nature, because it becomes part of a larger whole."[15] Because Mies in a next step asks viewers to perceive once again paintings, sculptures, and views of the landscape in direct connection, he explodes the ideal sphere of the work of art as an apparent alternative world and in effect relativizes its claim to autonomy, which was, after all, responsible for the rift.

The functional flaws of the Neue Nationalgalerie should be evaluated and their importance weighed against that backdrop. The inadequate lighting conditions on the lower story of the museum, where artificial and natural light necessarily transition fluidly, are based on the fundamental idea of an open museum as such. The all-glass wall facing the sculpture courtyard produces a close connection to the exterior and thus hampers the usual isolation of the gallery spaces. Gradual change in the lighting characterizes the transition of the lower level of the museum into a intimate exterior framed by walls, which not only provides a space to erect sculptures but also forms a scenic background for the paintings inside (fig. 4). Integrated into space and time, against the open sky and the vegetation outdoors, they are thus related to the cyclical change of the time of day and the seasons. The upper area of the museum, which according to the architectural program was intended for temporary exhibitions of contemporary art, evokes by contrast the urban context of the metropolis (fig. 5). The transparent walls of the large hall offer an open prospect across the terrace of the surroundings, which today, more than half a century after the building's completion, are essentially defined by the buildings of the Kulturforum. Even with closed curtains—Mies insisted that such protective measures only be adopted in the case of the immediate risk of direct sunlight[16]—the buildings still remain present as silhouettes (ill. pp. 76–77). Mies countered a one-sided, largely aesthetically oriented perspective that was necessarily provoked by conventional museum architecture with a maximum of "publicness" by bringing the city into the museum, so to speak. The concept of an open hall with no fixed subdivisions of the space thus inevitably involves a not inconsiderable limitation on the exhibition-makers. As Dirk Lohan stated in his speech on the occasion of the opening, Mies, too, was very much aware of that fact: "I know from Mies that it is completely clear to him that it will not always be easy to create good exhibitions in such a space. On the other hand, however, great opportunities exist that should not be forsaken."[17]

Let us summarize: the genesis of the design of the Neue Nationalgalerie was based on various fundamental concepts in the work of Mies van der Rohe that were initially developed separately from one another and were first brought together for the Schweinfurt project.[18] The integration of art and architecture was already a theme in his early work (Kröller-Müller design of 1912) and in the late 1930s was approaching a clarification that would be binding for Mies. Superficially independent of this problem, the result was the formal solution of an all-glass hall with no fixed spatial subdivisions on an only slightly elevated podium. Here, the point of departure was the Barcelona Pavilion of 1929. In the ideal project of the Fifty by Fifty Feet House of 1950–52 and finally in the unrealized Bacardi headquarters in Cuba, its context-related free grouping of masses gave way to a disposition of façades that is symmetrical on all sides, which only responds to the concrete connection to the place in the design of the exterior: the layout of the terrace, the open stairs, the facing masonry, and the plants.[19] The increasing abstraction from local conditions in his late work was the product of an effort that no longer sought the individual, single solution but rather strove to develop universally valid building types in harmony with a basic philosophical attitude concerned with balance. The hoped-for state of equilibrium—the higher unity of nature, human being, and architecture (with the inclusion of art, as one can surely add)—was now to be achieved while excluding all of the factors subject to chance. Because, however, a balanced yet asymmetrical group of masses can always produce only a relative, that is, unstable balance of forces, a return to static symmetry suggested itself. It alone provided a guarantee of producing the desired state of a perfect, absolute equilibrium—which even since Johann Joachim Winckelmann has been generally understood as "classical." That Mies also saw it that way is demonstrated by his own evaluation of the design for the Nationalgalerie: "The museum is, I believe, a classical solution to the task set for me . . . ."[20]

1 This essay is a slightly abridged and revised version of my essay "Die Neue Nationalgalerie im Werk Mies van der Rohes und im Kontext der Berliner Museumsarchitektur," in *Berlins Museen: Geschichte und Zukunft*, ed. Zentralinstitut für Kunstgeschichte München (Munich: Deutscher Kunstverlag, 1994), pp. 281–92. Of the literature that has appeared since, the following works particularly deserve mention: *Neue Nationalgalerie Berlin: Dreißig Jahre*, exh. cat. Neue Nationalgalerie, Berlin (Berlin: Paul Kahlfeldt, 1998), especially the essay by Dirk Lohan, "Skizzen der Erinnerung: Zum 30jährigen Jubiläum der Neuen Nationalgalerie, Berlin," pp. 7–12, as well as the discussions of Phyllis Lambert in *Mies in America*, ed. Phyllis Lambert, exh. cat. Canadian Centre for Architecture, Montreal, and Whitney Museum, New York (New York: Harry N. Abrams, 2001), pp. 475–99.

2 The agreement between the State of Berlin, as the party responsible for the Galerie des 20. Jahrhunderts, and the Stiftung Preussischer Kulturbesitz for the Nationalgalerie on a future merging of the two was signed on June 9, 1965, and was officially carried out on December 13, 1967. After the Stiftung took over the implementation of construction, the cornerstone ceremony followed on September 23, 1965.

3 Rolf Schwedler, the Senator for Building and Housing, to Ludwig Mies van der Rohe, July 6, 1961, Library of Congress, Washington, DC (hereafter LoC), Box VI, Folder 49: "I sincerely ask your forgiveness if I have not responded to your letter of April 7, 1961, in which you greeted the opportunity to accept a building project in our city. . . . Today, I would therefore merely like to let you know that I will be in Chicago from July 24 to 28 and would be very pleased if I could look you up and speak to you. We could then also discuss our ideas for a building designed by you . . . in the German capital." Over the course of further conversations, three projects were on the short list: "1. Museum plan on the site of the Schloss Charlottenburg [Charlottenburg Palace], 2. Developing a forum academicum for the Freie Universität in Dahlem, 3. Developing a cultural center on the site of Matthäikirchplatz and Kemperplatz"; Senate Director of Building Werner Düttmann to Ludwig Mies van der Rohe, October 31, 1961, LoC, Box III, Folder 18.

4 As will be shown, the reservations expressed at the time were already focused on the unfavorable lighting conditions in the upper exhibition hall and in the gallery spaces for the permanent collection in the basement; Werner Düttmann to Ludwig Mies van der Rohe, June 10 and November 13, 1963, LoC, Box III, Folder 19; of the museum experts he consulted at the time, Leopold Reidemeister, Adolf Jannasch, Arnold Bode, and, later in the process, Werner Haftmann and Stephan Waetzoldt can be identified by name.

5 Werner Düttmann to Ludwig Mies van der Rohe, January 22, 1962, LoC, Box III, Folder 18, mentions a space allocation program that was said to have been discussed with Adolf Jannasch, the director of the Galerie des 20. Jahrhunderts.

6 Stephan Waetzoldt, "Planung für die Museen am Tiergarten," *Jahrbuch Preussischer Kulturbesitz* 9 (1971), pp. 35–45, esp. pp. 35ff.

7 On this, see also Stephan Waetzoldt, "Mies van der Rohes 'Neue Nationalgalerie'," in *Nationalgalerie Berlin: 10 Jahre im neuen Haus*, exh. cat. Wissenschaftszentrum, Bonn-Bad Godesberg (Berlin: SMB, 1978), pp. 8–10.

8 On the residential projects mentioned above and below, see Wolf Tegethoff, *Mies van der Rohe: Die Villen und Landhausprojekte* (Essen: Bacht, 1981).

9 For more detail on this, see Wolf Tegethoff, "Die Entwicklung der Raumauffassung im Werk Mies van der Rohes," *Daidalos* (September 13, 1984), pp. 114–23.

10 The dating to 1941 or 1942 frequently encountered in pertinent literature—most recently in *The Mies van der Rohe Archive: An Illustrated Catalogue of the Mies van der Rohe Drawings in the Museum of Modern Art*, part 2 (1938–1967), ed. Franz Schulze with George Danforth, vol. 13 (New York: Garland, 1992), p. 68—finds no support in the sparse surviving sources at MoMA; see also Phyllis Lambert, "Project for a Museum for a Small City (1943)," in Lambert, *Mies in America*, pp. 426–29.

11 Howard Myers to Ludwig Mies van der Rohe, telegram, February 3, 1943, MoMA.

12 Ludwig Mies van der Rohe to Howard Myers, copy of a telegram, n.d., MoMA.

13 Revised version of the explanatory report by Mies, sent to George Nelson on April 9, 1943, MoMA. The wooden English of the manuscript, which for documentary reasons was preferred here over the published version, makes it clear that Mies van der Rohe was its author. It was published in *Architectural Forum* 78, no. 5 (May 1943), pp. 84–85.

14 The commission was probably mediated by Dirk Lohan, grandson of Mies van der Rohe and son-in-law of Georg Schäfer, who after completing his studies of architecture in Munich in the early 1960s joined the office of his grandfather (correspondence in the Mies van der Rohe Archive, MoMA). Lohan was, alongside and after Gene Summers, crucially involved in the planning and building of the Neue Nationalgalerie.

15 Quoted in Christian Norberg-Schulz, "Talks with Mies van der Rohe," *L'architecture d'aujourd'hui* 29, no. 79 (September 1958), p. 100.

16 Dirk Lohan to Werner Haftmann, October 22, 1968, LoC, Box III, Folder 24: "The curtain in the exhibition hall should truly only be closed when solar radiation presents an absolute risk to the art objects. After all, especially from outside, the curtain represents a very direct spatial termination."

17 Manuscript of Dirk Lohan's opening speech, LoC, Box III, Folder 21.

18 The set of plans for the Neue Nationalgalerie preserves several drawings that deviate considerably from the design that was implemented: MoMA 6204.12 shows a cantilever roof over the hall on a single, enormous central pillar; MoMA 6204.63, for which an elaborate model also exists, offers a solution with flashed supports similar to the type in Crown Hall at the IIT; the model is reproduced in Schulze and Danforth, *An Illustrated Catalogue of the Mies van der Rohe Drawings in the Museum of Modern Art*, part 2, vol. 19, p. 152. As Dirk Lohan confirmed in a conversation with the author, these were works from the studio, usually by the hand of Gene Summers, created during an extended hospital stay by Mies, which then he rejected immediately on his return. It cannot be ruled out, however, that in an early planning stage, and before the Schweinfurt commission was returned, alternative solutions for Berlin were tried out. For a detailed account of the planning history, see Lohan, "Skizzen der Erinnerung: Zum 30jährigen Jubiläum der Neuen Nationalgalerie, Berlin," and Lambert, *Mies in America*. By contrast, there was a serious discussion for a time about expanding the terrace to the west with a sculpture courtyard that would have been wrapped around all sides of the gallery spaces; MoMA 6204.11, 6204.23, 6204.60, and 6204.62; see also the model in Schulze and Danforth, *An Illustrated Catalogue*, part 2, vol. 19, p. 153, which would have noticeably improved the lighting in parts of the subterranean floor: "We are working on two models studying the court position . . ."; Gene Summers to Werner Düttmann, July 26, 1963, LoC, Box III, Folder 19. This can probably be traced back to a suggestion by Arnold Bode—see Werner Düttmann to Ludwig Mies van der Rohe, June 10, 1963, LoC, Box III, Folder 18—but in the end it was not pursued; see Ludwig Mies van der Rohe to Werner Düttmann, September 13, 1963, LoC, Box III, Folder 19: "The last proposal made to cut the museum garden out of the terrace seems to me to be the most important one. . . . We too had that solution in mind in the beginning; it very clearly has certain advantages; it allows for more exhibition space and more daylight. At the same time, however, it trivializes the architectural idea. The museum garden does not seem to me to be half as good with glass walls framing it, and the idea of the terrace would be watered down by its excessive dimensions. I believe that the decision to be made here is an architectural one. Our decision is clearer, better defined, and is simply better architecturally."

19 By contrast, I have tried to show elsewhere just how much the disposition of masses of the Barcelona Pavilion was determined by the topographical and architectural situation of the exhibition site; see Tegethoff, *Mies van der Rohe: Die Villen und Landhausprojekte*, pp. 87ff.

20 Ludwig Mies van der Rohe to Werner Düttmann, February 26, 1963, LoC, Box III, Folder 19.

The Transparency

Exhibitionist Architecture: Looking through Mies

Beatriz Colomina

A photograph taken during the construction of the Neue Nationalgalerie in Berlin shows Ludwig Mies van der Rohe looking through the window of a white car as the massive one-piece 1,250 ton steel roof of the building was raised into position (ill. p. 2). According to Dirk Lohan, his grandson, collaborator, and the driver of the car, "When the roof was at a level of two meters, Mies determined to walk under it to see if the space emerging corresponded to his idea of what it should look like. I accompanied him as he walked with great difficulty beneath the floating roof."[1] It was April 5, 1967. Another photograph on the same day shows the figure of Mies with a coat and a hat on, propped with two canes and holding a briefcase as he appears to prepare to cross the street to see the building from the other side (fig. 6 top, p. 62). This was his last view of the building. Mies had traveled to Berlin for this occasion but was too fragile to come back again for the festivities of the ceremonial opening on September 15, 1968. He died on August 17, 1969, without seeing the building completed.

Or had he seen it completed already? Seen, that is the key polemical statement—the space between the two massive horizontals that would eventually be lightly contained by huge panes of glass yet barely transformed by them, as if emptiness had been placed in a vitrine, a kind of display case, offering it to the city in a dramatic gesture of exposure. So exposed, in fact, that the building at first doesn't seem to have an inside. Even from a distance there is the uncanny sense that what normally would be an inside is oddly bigger than the outside, that Berlin has expanded, as if through a lens. The Neue Nationalgalerie is not so much a building in Berlin as a way of seeing Berlin and of becoming yourself the exhibit. Transparency here is, anyway, never simple.

The photographs of the Neue Nationalgalerie under construction recall the image of Mies around 1950 in front of the structure of the Farnsworth House in Plano, Illinois, where his lonely figure appears to somberly appraise the empty frame (fig. 1). His enormous stature cuts a black silhouette into the frigid landscape. With his coat and hat on, and his back to the camera, he stands like one of Caspar David Friedrich's figures confronting the sublime. Here, again, there is the uncanny sense that the landscape has been expanded by an "almost nothing" lens of two horizontal planes that will receive only the most delicate shimmery distortions of the barest glass curtain to mark the limit of an occupiable viewing instrument. This is a house not a museum and yet there is a palpable sense of exhibition. Firstly, the house itself is on exhibit—shockingly different from everything around it, just as the Neue Nationalgalerie defines itself in opposition to the city around it. Secondly, the smooth, perfected floating geometry of both buildings suggests that they have just landed from outer space and paradoxically render everything around them as an exotic captivating landscape on exhibit. Thirdly, everything seen within the spaces is on show. But the ultimate exhibitionism is the combination of all three: the view through the building. The eye passing through the structure is aware that the lens is there, but it focuses only on the distant landscape. Mies's architecture is never simply an object sitting there in its perfection, waiting for us to look at it. It waits to be looked through and, in that moment, becomes out of focus, even ghostly. When Mies looked through a building, and when we, too, look through it, then we complete the work, even become a part of it.

Seeing through architecture. This is the effect that Mies tried to produce in the work—the effect that, again and again, he checked in buildings under construction, but also in the models. For example, in the glass models he built of the Glass Skyscraper project of 1922, where he realized that the important thing in glass architecture "is the play of reflections and not the effect of light and shadow, as in ordinary buildings."[2] He repeatedly photographed these models in a garden in Berlin before arriving at the few canonic images he finally released. During the opening of his first solo exhibition, at MoMA in 1947, before the Farnsworth House was completed, Mies is seen in a photograph bending over a pedestal, looking intently through the model of the house on exhibit. Not at the model but through it, as if to demonstrate what is important, or even to check the optical effect (fig. 2).

Architecture is a lens through which to see the world, and therefore it has to almost disappear in order to give way to this view. In the Neue Nationalgalerie, all of the elements of the building are thinned down or buried in the plinth so

1 Ludwig Mies van der Rohe on the construction site of the Farnsworth House, 1950

that the structure offers the minimum definition and the works of art displayed will define a different architecture for each temporary exhibition. Depthless collages of suspended panels communicate the essence of the building even though the building itself does not appear in the collages, except for the most delicate grid lines (fig. 3). The collages stage an act of looking through the volume to the courtyard and the trees beyond. Even the art is seen not directly but off to the side of an eye that is uninterrupted as it moves through and out. The architecture is not even a frame. Or at least not a frame for art. Photographs show, even before the first exhibition was hung, the plain white panels suspended from the ceiling, designed to support paintings, acting in fact as minimalist paintings in their own right but not blocking the eye that can keep moving under, over, or past them (ill. pp. 68–69).

But if looking through is what makes the building, then the opening that Mies missed was the inauguration of this unique way of viewing. In the photographs, the visitors spread out to the edges of the site, moving restlessly and looking at everything except the architecture and the art. They look through the spaces at each other, from the plinth through the main gallery, from the gallery to the courtyard (ill. p. 70), and so on. They go into the building only to pass through and look back through.

Looking at the photographs of the opening, I am touched by the sense of domesticity. This was not the usual stiff affair of a museum opening with people gravely observing the artworks or the building, but an almost wild party with guests dancing to the beat of live music of the Dixieland band in the courtyard (figs. 4, 5). Bodies moving in space, close together, drinking, talking, laughing, some dancing, others perched on the edge of the plinth looking down to the party in the courtyard below (fig. 6). The museum feels like a big house with a patio. The view through, the feeling when architecture goes out of focus, produces a new sense of shared release.

In the case of the Neue Nationalgalerie, Mies's logic of exhibiting without foregrounding—as if teasing the view with what is just off to one side or with a kind of mirage in the distance—becomes everything in the most public of

2 Ludwig Mies van der Rohe in front of the model of the Farnsworth House, 1947

3 Opening exhibition, *Piet Mondrian*, 1968

4 Opening ceremony of the Neue Nationalgalerie, September 15, 1968

5 Dixieland band in the sculpture garden for the opening ceremony, 1968

buildings, but at the same time it retains its domesticity. The building is a hybrid of the glass house and the courtyard house. In the photographs of the opening, people are behaving as if in the garden of a big house. And they, too, are on exhibit. Upstairs in the pavilion they float in space like the paintings, and the walls hold them lightly, even tenderly (ill. p. 95). The miracle of Mies's architecture is that you are continuously framed and reframed in different ways. From the front, the side, just your legs . . . And the reverse is also true. The art seems a visitor as well, one that may leave before you do.

The Neue Nationalgalerie in Berlin, now in the fifty-third year of its life, is Mies van der Rohe's last building, and in a sense also his first. It is as if Mies only ever had one project, reworked endlessly on different sites, a single experiment with a new kind of transparency, a new way of exhibiting the world—an experiment that began and ended in Berlin. When making a gallery, Mies was not simply making a space for exhibitions. All his work is exhibitionist. Mies was incubated in the immaterial space of exhibitions, and he ultimately absorbed the logic of exhibition into the very material of his architecture.

If the Neue Nationalgalerie is a big house, then Mies van der Rohe and Lilly Reich had repeatedly stretched the concept of exhibition into that of the house since the 1920s. For example, when the German Glass Industry commissioned a display of their products for the exhibition *Die Wohnung* (The Dwelling) in Stuttgart in 1927, the two architects turned their *Glasraum* (Glass Room) display into a house, a flowing space subdivided into a dining room, living room, and workroom by freestanding glass walls (fig. 8). The illusion of a ceiling was produced by strips of stretched fabric; the floors were covered with white, gray, red, and black linoleum areas that produced a sense of movement by not quite coinciding with the rooms; the walls were of etched, clear, and gray opaque glass; the chairs were covered in white chamois and black cowhide; and the bench table was in rosewood.[3] Even a sense of the outside was produced by placing plants and a sculpture of a woman on the other side of one of the glass walls. This strategy anticipates the Barcelona Pavilion, Mies's most famous project.

6 1,200 invited guests celebrated the opening of the Neue Nationalgalerie, 1968

7 Speeches and conversations during the opening ceremony, 1968

When commissioned to build the German Pavilion for the Barcelona International Exposition in 1929, Mies asked the German Ministry of Foreign Affairs what was to be exhibited. "Nothing will be exhibited," he was told, "the pavilion itself will be the exhibit."[4] In the absence of a traditional client or program, Mies was able to take his work to new limits, and one of the most influential buildings of the century emerged. Once again, Mies and Reich, who collaborated on the project, had taken the opportunity to make a proto-house (fig. 9). Defined by the strategic placement of sensuous materials, its flowing space continued the investigations started with the Brick Country House and the Glass Room in Stuttgart. Even the presence of a Georg Kolbe sculpture of a nude woman in the Glass Room would reappear in the *Deutsche Bauausstellung* (German Building Exhibition) in Berlin two years later, when the experiment continued.

Exhibitions in the twentieth century acted as sites for the incubation of new forms of architecture that were sometimes so shockingly original, so new, that they were not even recognized as architecture at all. Think, for example, about the Barcelona Pavilion, widely understood in the architectural world today as the most influential building of the twentieth century. It was in fact seen by "nobody." Despite its prominent location in the layout of the 1929 International Exposition in Barcelona, even journalists sent by professional architectural magazines passed it over entirely, unable to detect its significance. Local journalists provided the only testimony to its existence. They commented on the "mysterious" effect, "because a person standing in front of one of these glass walls sees himself reflected as if by a mirror, but if he moves behind them, he then sees the exterior perfectly [fig. 10]. Not all the visitors notice this curious particularity whose cause remains ignored."[5] It is necessary to go back to these kinds of statements to understand the surprise that a glass building produced in 1929, something that, as Alison Smithson put it, a generation that has grown up around glassy Hilton International hotels may have difficulty imagining.

It was only in the 1950s, in the aftermath of the 1947–48 exhibition *Mies van der Rohe* at the Museum of Modern Art in New York, that the Barcelona Pavilion burst into every architectural publication.[6] As glass architecture became dominant, the pavilion was hailed as the most beautiful building of the century, exemplifying the cult of transparency. A building that was known only through magazine images (it was dismantled at the closing of the exhibition in Barcelona and its fragments misplaced during its return trip to Germany) became the most significant monument of modern architecture. Retroactively, the pavilion is seen to exemplify the new optical and spatial freedom embodied in Mies's houses and exported to all building types.

What is crucial about the Barcelona Pavilion is that it was both real, a one-to-one structure that existed for a time, and an image, a media construction. All we knew about it, before its reconstruction in 1986, were the photographs. It lived in the photographs. The images capture the sense of looking through, from outside to inside to outside. The plan seems to multiply the opportunities for views through. The photographs are not simply of an object, but of a way of viewing supported by an object. The ambiguities produced by the reflections in the glass extend to the object. Even when the looking through does not pass through glass, the seemingly sharp forms are softened by our concentration on the spaces in the distance.

Again and again, Mies constructs an object that is ultimately meant to give way to the view it makes possible. Take the Tugendhat House (1928–30), for example, which sits on a sloping site. The house blocks the view from the street, except for an opening which frames a small fragment—a postcard view—which both lures you in and keeps you at a distance with the railing (fig. 11). This framed picture defines the entrance space of the house. It protects you, encloses you, as much as the overhang does, by keeping the "outside" at a distance. And it is only when already inside the house, having to pass down the spiral staircase, that the panoramic view finally becomes possible through a glass wall, which can be made to disappear into the floor with the help of a complex machine. Shelter in Mies's houses, protection from the outside, is provided by a window's ability to turn the threatening world outside the home into a reassuring picture. The inhabitant is enveloped, wrapped, protected by the pictures. These perspectives are not simply neutral views of

8 Ludwig Mies van der Rohe and Lilly Reich, *Die Wohnung* (The Dwelling), Deutsche Werkbund exhibition, Stuttgart, 1927

9 Barcelona Pavilion by Ludwig Mies van der Rohe on the opening day, May 27, 1929, with King Alfonso XIII of Spain

10 Ludwig Mies van der Rohe, Barcelona Pavilion, 1929

11 Ludwig Mies van der Rohe, Tugendhat House, Brünn (now Brno), Czechoslovakia, 1930

the outside world. The world is at once turned into an outside and interrogated, intensified, transformed, by being framed. As Mies puts it: "When one looks at Nature through the glass walls of the Farnsworth House it takes on a deeper significance than when one stands outside. More is asked for from Nature, because it becomes part of a greater whole."[7] The glass house doesn't simply expose the exterior world. It actively turns the world into a highly composed display. Symptomatic in that respect is Fritz Tugendhat's response to the architectural critic Justus Bier, who had polemically asked the question "Is the Tugendhat house habitable?" in the pages of the journal *Die Form*:[8] "After almost a year of living in the house, I can assure you without hesitation that technically it possesses everything a modern person might wish for . . . . On clear and frosty days, one can lower its windows, sit in the sun, and enjoy the view of a snow-covered landscape, like Davos."[9] The house itself has perceptually disappeared. What makes the Tugendhat habitable is the view through it. Habitation means occupying this view.

The glass house represented the realization of the century-old dream of a transparent house. This dream extended from the science-fiction-like quality of Paul Scheerbart's images of glass buildings in an ideal future in his novels and in his 1914 collection of aphorisms *Glasarchitektur* (published in English as *Glass Architecture*), dedicated to Bruno Taut, to Taut's own *Glashaus* (the pavilion for the glass industry in the German Werkbund exhibition in Cologne of 1914), to Mies van der Rohe and Lilly Reich's Glass Room in Stuttgart of 1927, and to Mies's German Pavilion at the 1929 Barcelona International Exposition and his project for a Glass House on a Hillside of 1934. By 1949, this dream of a house defined only by glass walls—or, we could even say, the absence of walls—was fully realized in the Farnsworth House. The spaceship had landed, or rather was floating just above the ground as if coming in to land (fig. 12). What had been experimented with in drawings, models, writings, and pavilions in fairs had finally become useful.

Already in 1947, in his book on Mies accompanying the exhibition at the Museum of Modern Art, Philip Johnson had described the Farnsworth House as "a floating self-contained cage"[10] and Henry-Russell Hitchcock described it as a "beached yacht" with no provisions for outer living beyond the very confined space of the fly-screened "deck" and the small travertine "dock" below it.[11] The idea of floating can already be found in early articles in the popular press, as when *House & Garden* magazine calls the house a "glass shell that 'floats' in the air."[12] It is this floating, disengaged quality that allows the house to take the logic of the exhibition out into the landscape. The house exposes everything, turning everything into a display, including itself. The house literally stages an exhibition for its occupants and becomes part of the show. The house turns the exhibition gallery inside out. The world itself is put on exhibit. This all-pervasive logic of the exhibition was a part of Mies's project from the beginning, which was always the attempt to assemble a house through an act of collection and exhibition.

Not by chance, many clients of Mies were prominent art collectors: Hugo Perls, for whom Mies built a house in Berlin in 1911–12, collected Pablo Picasso, Henri Matisse, and Edvard Munch; Helene Müller, who commissioned the unrealized project for the Kröller-Müller Villa in the Netherlands in 1912–13, was a formidable art collector (fifty Vincent van Gogh paintings alone had to be accommodated in the plans of the project); Eric Wolf, the client of Mies's first modern house, had a great collection of Caspar David Friedrich, Adolph von Menzel, and German Expressionist art; Hermann Lange, who commissioned Mies to do a house for him in Krefeld, was a collector of Cubist and German Expressionist art; Karl Lemke, the client of Mies's only completed court house, was a printer and art collector. But perhaps the most paradigmatic of Mies's client/collectors was Eduard Fuchs, the protagonist of Walter Benjamin's essay "Eduard Fuchs, Collector and Historian" (1931), who bought the house of Hugo Perls in 1927 and commissioned Mies to do an extension to accommodate his collection.

In fact, most of Mies's clients—whether bankers, lawyers, or industrialists—were amateur art collectors, and Mies always made proposals for how to hang their art, considering the placement of works of art as part of the house design. It is important to remember that Mies himself was also an amateur art collector who acquired, over the course of his life, more than forty works of art (twenty-two by Paul Klee,

12 Ludwig Mies van der Rohe, Farnsworth House, Plano, Illinois, 1980

13 Ludwig Mies van der Rohe in his apartment in Chicago, Illinois, 1964

14 Ludwig Mies van der Rohe, Resor House, view out into the surroundings, collage, 1937–38

fourteen by Kurt Schwitters, and some by Max Beckmann, Wassily Kandinsky, and Pablo Picasso).[13] Most of the works in his collection were small, and he used them in his domestic settings (fig. 13). Not having any savings, Mies used to say that his collection was his life insurance.

It was yet another art collector, Helen Resor, who brought Mies to the United States. She was a trustee of The Museum of Modern Art (MoMA) who had been introduced to Mies's work by the museum's director, Alfred H. Barr. In the controversy over who should design the new MoMA, Barr was in favor of Mies, while Nelson Rockefeller preferred Philip Goodwin and Edward Durell Stone. Resor was on Barr's side despite the fact that she was a client of Goodwin's, who had already built a small guest cabin at Resor's ranch in Jackson Hole, Wyoming. In support of Barr, she fired Goodwin and commissioned Mies to do a house at the ranch.[14]

Resor was a force. She was the director of the world's largest international advertising agency (the J. Walter Thompson company) and a legendary copywriter, famous for coining the phrase "A skin you love to touch" for the advertising campaign of Woodbury's Facial Soap. She was also innovative with images that transformed the look of advertising. She hired Edward Steichen, later the director of MoMA's photography department, on an exclusive contract in 1924. She put together innovative advertising campaigns introducing new products to American consumers (Cutex nail polish, Lever Brothers' Lux soap, etc.). If MoMA was trying to repackage modern architecture for an American audience, then Helen Resor had all the expertise to do it. Mies was simply the next product to be imported, displayed, and promoted.

Resor was a brilliant fundraiser at MoMA and made a financial agreement with Barr so she could buy art in Europe for MoMA without restrictions. She would keep whatever MoMA didn't take on the understanding that the museum could buy it later at the original price. Even the importing of Mies seems to have followed that pattern. In the end, MoMA went for Goodwin and Durrell Stone, while Resor kept Mies. She even personally brought Mies over from Europe, traveling back to the United States with him by ocean liner, arriving in New York in August 1937. Resor wanted to fly to her ranch in Wyoming (United Airlines being one of her advertising clients) but Mies refused, preferring to take the train via Chicago.[15]

Back in New York, Mies worked for six months on the design of the Resor House, producing over 800 drawings. The basic idea was to create a bridge with the sense of an open box floating in the air. Goodwin had already decided the location over a small river and installed a set of concrete piers to support the house. Mies's project used the same piers and thinned all the elements down to create a large glass room suspended in the air (fig. 14). Much of the endless redrawing of the project attempts to position floating walls in the space, culminating in a famous collage where the view through the expansive glass wall is transformed into a new kind of space (fig. 2, p. 82). The deep view toward the distant mountains that the site makes available has been replaced with a still from a Western movie facing a steep hillside. It reads like a depthless flat screen with a set of floating panels in the foreground. One of the panels, an enlarged reproduction of Paul Klee's *Bunte Mahlzeit* (Colorful Meal)—a painting in Resor's collection, purchased during Mies's stay in New York and probably with his advice—becomes a freestanding element, juxtaposed with a wood veneer panel in the foreground that has the same proportions as the landscape view. The view offered by the house is no longer a direct exposure to the outside. Rather, the outside is reframed, brought inside, and transformed into a large painting or, more precisely, a cinematic frame. The collages are again polemically sharp, but the building is almost out of the picture, and even the artworks are to the side of the view that passes through. Mies produced high-resolution images of a way of blurring both architecture and art in favor of a sensuous encounter with the distance. The interior is a landscape that gives way to the extended landscape beyond.

The pivotal project was cancelled in 1938, but Mies kept working on it, presenting new models and drawings of the house in his 1947 exhibition at MoMA. The concept of transforming the status of both art and architecture led directly to his Museum for a Small City (1942, fig. 3, p. 82), a project which stands with Le Corbusier's Museum of Unlimited Growth (1931) as the two most significant proposals for museums of the modern movement.

The Museum for a Small City was the result of a commission from the journal *Architectural Forum* to design a church for a special issue of the magazine dedicated to "New Buildings for 194X" to be published in 1943. Mies, who had been tutoring George Danforth, a student doing a museum thesis, suggested to *Architectural Forum* that instead of a church he would design a museum. Danforth had worked on the Resor collages and was testing the same strategy on a larger scale.[16] The collages of the museum are very similar to those of the Resor House. Paintings and sculptures are used in the museum as if they were walls and columns defining a space with the feeling of the outdoors. For Mies, the main point was not to contain the art within the architecture, but to use the art to create architecture. In his text for *Architectural Forum,* Mies wrote: "The first problem is to establish the museum as a center for the enjoyment, not the internment of art. In this project the barrier between the art work and the living community is erased by a garden approach for the display of sculpture. Interior sculptures enjoy an equal spatial freedom, because the open plan permits them to be seen against the surrounding hills. The architectural space, thus achieved, becomes a defining rather than a confining space. A work such as Picasso's *Guernica* has been difficult to place in the usual museum gallery. Here it can be shown to greatest advantage and become an element in space against a changing background."[17]

Art for Mies was a spatial element, but once again supporting a way of viewing rather than simply being viewed. In the Museum for a Small City, *Guernica* becomes a freestanding wall. As in the Resor House, in collages and similar images for the earlier Court House projects, all of the traditional elements of architecture—floor, walls, ceilings, and columns—are barely delineated or simply invisible. It is the unrestrained art that takes over in constructing a visual depth. The works on exhibit generate the real architecture that is occupied. Mies's architecture had been incubated in the gallery space from the beginning. His work is an optical instrument, born in temporary display spaces, then unleashed in different landscapes around the world.

One notices, when looking again at all of Mies's canonical works, that they are exhibitionistic in character. It is not just that they are designed to be published, or designed to photograph well. Rather, they are concerned with new forms of exposure, new forms of display, new forms of transparency. The object has been deeply affected by the fact that it is both constructed in the media and infiltrated by the media. Always on show, it has become thoroughly exhibitionist.

This relentless strategy continued in the project for the unbuilt Bacardi headquarters in Santiago, Cuba (1957–60, fig. 2, p. 58), which became the final model for the Neue Nationalgalerie in Berlin (1962–68). Mies's one extended project finally returned to Berlin as the ultimate statement of an architecture designed to be looked through—a new kind of transparency where the object slips out of view in the very moment that it supports the view that passes through.

1 Dirk Lohan, "Skizzen der Erinnerung," in *Neue Nationalgalerie Berlin: Dreißig Jahre*, ed. Paul Kahlfeldt and Andres Lepik (Berlin: Staatliche Museen zu Berlin, 1998), p. 11. See the text by Dirk Lohan in the present volume.
2 Ludwig Mies van der Rohe, *Frühlicht* 1, no. 4 (1922), quoted in Philip Johnson, *Mies van der Rohe* (1947; repr., New York: MoMA, 1978), p. 187.
3 Franz Schulze, *Mies van der Rohe: A Critical Biography* (Chicago and London: University of Chicago Press, 1985), pp. 141–42. Matilda McQuaid, *Lilly Reich: Designer and Architect*, exh. cat. Museum of Modern Art, New York (New York: Abrams, 1996), p. 25. The exhibition was on show from February 7 to May 7, 1996.
4 Julius Posener, "Los primeros años: de Schinkel a De Stijl," *A&V: Monografías de Arquitectura y Vivienda* 6, special issue on Mies van der Rohe (1986), pp. 24–35, esp. p. 33.
5 A journalist from Barcelona reviewing the pavilion, quoted in Josep Quetglas, *Der gläserne Schrecken: Imágenes del Pabellón de Alemania* (Montreal: Les Éditions Section B, 1991), p. 48. Published in English as: Josep Quetglas, "Fear of Glass: The Barcelona Pavilion," in *Revisions* 2, ed. Beatriz Colomina (New York: Princeton Architectural Press, 1988), p. 130.
6 Juan Pablo Bonta, *Architecture and Its Interpretation: A Study of Expressive Systems in Architecture* (New York: Rizzoli International, 1979), pp. 131–74.
7 Ludwig Mies van der Rohe in conversation with Christian Norberg-Schulz, in *Baukunst und Werkform* 11 (November 1958).
8 Justus Bier, "Kann man im Haus Tugendhat wohnen?," *Die Form* 6, no. 10 (October 15, 1931), pp. 392–93, esp. p. 392.
9 Fritz Tugendhat, "Das Haus Tugendhat," *Die Form* 6, no. 11 (November 15, 1931), pp. 437–38.
10 Johnson, *Mies van der Rohe*, p. 162.
11 Henry-Russell Hitchcock, "The Current Work of Philip Johnson," *Zodiac 8: International Magazine of Contemporary Architecture* (1961), pp. 64–81, esp. p. 66.
12 "A Glass Shell that 'Floats' in the Air," in *House & Garden*, February 1952.
13 For a detailed account of Mies's collection, see Vivian Endicott Barnett, "The Architect as Collector," in *Mies in America*, ed. Phyllis Lambert, exh. cat. Canadian Centre for Architecture, Montreal, and Whitney Museum, New York (New York: Harry N. Abrams, 2001), pp. 90–131.
14 See Cammie McAtee, "Alien #5044325: Mies' First Trip to America," in Lambert, *Mies in America*, pp. 132–91.
15 Ibid.
16 For a year or so, George Danforth had been experimenting with collages of large artworks defining a public gallery. One day, says Danforth, he walked into the office and Mies was smiling with a telegram in his hand. "He said: 'Ja, shall we do it?' And that stopped my work on the thesis." Kevin Harrington in conversation with George Danforth, quoted in Phyllis Lambert, "Space and Structure," in *Mies in America*, pp. 332–521, esp. p. 426.
17 Ludwig Mies van der Rohe, "Museum for a Small City," *Architectural Forum* 78, no. 5 (May 1943), pp. 84–85. Reprinted in Fritz Neumeyer, *The Artless Word: Mies van der Rohe on the Building Art*, trans. Mark Jarzombek (Cambridge, MA: The MIT Press, 1991), p. 322.

The Space

Joachim Jäger

The dream of open, universally usable space was first fulfilled in Chicago. In the 1950s—long before the distinguished invitation to build a museum in Berlin was sent to Mies van der Rohe—planning in Chicago had provided the German-born architect with crucial new impulses. A commission from the City of Chicago to redesign completely a large university campus for the Illinois Institute of Technology enabled Mies to refine very different visionary building types he had already imagined elsewhere. This is particularly true of his long-pursued idea of universal space: a space that was clearly framed but was meant to be broadly and openly arranged at the same time—a space that was intended for many different uses. With Crown Hall (1950–56), the building for architecture and urban planning that stood crosswise to the campus, Mies was able to make that idea a reality on a monumental scale for the first time (fig. 1, p. 58). Four large steel beams that mightily surround the building bear a broad, pillarless hall of dimensions that were impressive at the time: 67 by 37 meters. The interior had no built-in furniture and was conceived flexibly, articulated only by low, rectangular, wooden cubicles and two stairways. In the design, broad areas are not defined precisely but instead identified as "open regions."[1] The building shell is also open, with windows all around: a light-flooded hall. The concise summary of this structure by the Swiss architect Werner Blaser, offered already in the 1950s, is apt: "It is not the building that is the work of art but the space."[2]

Mies van der Rohe had previously grappled with the idea of large expanses of space in important studies. *Project for a Concert Hall* (1942), presented as a collage, and *Project for a Drive-in-Restaurant* (1945–48) are particularly worthy of mention. Both are attempts to open up large interiors to the outside as much as possible. In the study for a concert hall, one side of the broad interior is even entirely delimited and hence open (fig. 1).[3] This play between a freedom that makes large spaces possible and boundaries that restrict and "define" these spaces was to become a guiding theme for Mies in the years that followed. On the occasion of his design Museum for a Small City (1943), he declared with great foresight of his own work: "The architectural space becomes a defining rather than a confining space."[4]

1 Ludwig Mies van der Rohe, Project for a Concert Hall, collage, 1942

2 Ludwig Mies van der Rohe, Toronto-Dominion Centre, 1973

3 *Franz Erhard Walther* exhibition, Neue Nationalgalerie, 1977

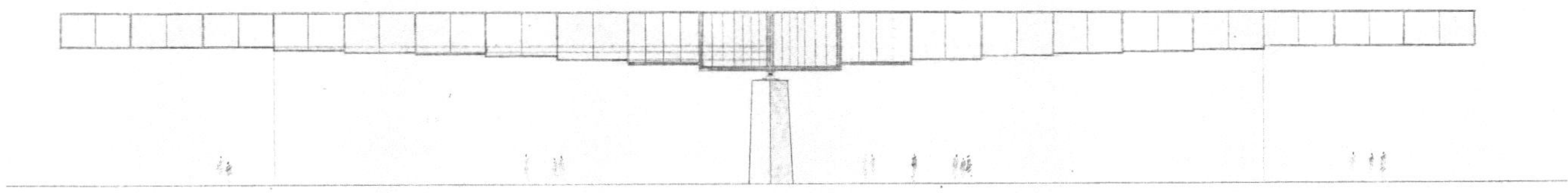

4 Ludwig Mies van der Rohe, Neue Nationalgalerie, preliminary study, 1960s

How such spaces could be created—on the one hand, as open as possible and, on the other, indeed "defined"—was famously explored by Mies on his path to the Neue Nationalgalerie using the example of two other prominent pavilion buildings: the Federal Center in Chicago (a public post office, begun in 1959) and the Toronto-Dominion Centre (a bank building, 1963–69, fig. 2). Both buildings take up the idea of Crown Hall—the concept of a broad, spanned interior—with distinct solutions for the constructions and proportions. Clearly recognizable—and emphasized by many authors on Mies—is the path of radicalization and simplification that he was diligently pursuing in this period.[5] The supports of the architecture are moved ever farther apart; the façades opened up more; the furnishings reduced to a minimum to achieve as much open space in the interior as possible.

All of these reflections ultimately culminated in the glass hall of the Neue Nationalgalerie, in this one large space that is open on four sides and transparent. The glass-and-steel façade became narrower and more thin-skinned by further reducing the structure between the windows. At the same time, Mies increased the overall building volume, almost monumentalizing the experience of space. To do so, he increased the dimensions of the windowpanes—also in comparison to the precursor designs (for the Bacardi company in Cuba and the Schäfer collection in Schweinfurt). The broadly projecting terrace, which features the same stone floor covering as the hall, results in a sliding continuum of space in all four directions. The space of this building begins, in essence, entirely outdoors, on the terrace, which is to be understood as an extended museum space. One already senses here the energy field of the light-flooded glass hall even before finally entering Mies's sphere beneath the heavy roof.

Phyllis Lambert therefore speaks of an "immersive" experience of this architecture, as is especially true of the glass hall, which despite its cloakrooms and supply shafts seems at first glance to lack all function.[6] It is a large, difficult-to-grasp exhibition space, precisely because it lacks anything like a foyer in front. On the floor plan of the presentation portfolio of 1963, Mies had originally drawn in a small counter that articulates the hall into a reception zone and an exhibition zone.[7] Nevertheless, the motif of a flowing, open space continued to be very determinant. Already in his design Museum for a Small City, Mies spoke of erasing "the barrier between the art work and the living community" and saw the works of art as "element[s] in space against a changing background."[8] With the Neue Nationalgalerie, this vision was fulfilled on a scale as large as could be imagined at the time. Even today, the height and breadth of the hall, with the strong connection outward into urban space, offer an impressive experience. Famously, Mies refused to accept any practical, technical, and other objections to this transparency and openness. He spoke of free space or a "stage" for art.[9]

The broadly jutting roof, which emphasizes the horizontal direction of the building, and the pellucid windows reinforce the motif of connecting interior and exterior. In many years of its use thus far, this potential of the hall has hardly been exploited at all. There are very few exhibitions that have thematized the way this space flows or have extended inside out, toward the terrace, for example. The artist Franz Erhard Walther, who did us the service of being the first to make productive use of the spaciousness of the glass hall, deliberately presented his performative works in interior and exterior spaces in equal measure (ill. p. 104). The works of Matt Mullican, Jenny Holzer, Douglas Gordon, and Keith Sonnier were very much designed with their effect on the outside in mind. In by far the majority of exhibitions, however, the motif of open and fluid space is not used much or at all. Why is that so? What does it say about the nature of the space?

An early sketch from Mies van der Rohe's office showing the roof construction of the Neue Nationalgalerie is revealing: it makes it clear how far they were ready to go in Chicago in thinking about the openness of the building (fig. 4). In this impressive study, the architecture is entirely reduced to a floating roof; the interior is delimited from its surroundings only by a delicate line. Mies van der Rohe's office was moving close to later ideas for the planning of open spaces and forums like those created, for example, by Frei Otto with his broadly spanning glass roof for the Expo 1967 in Montreal or for the roof of the stadium for the Olympics in Munich in 1972. In his final design for the Neue Nationalgalerie, by contrast, Mies consciously returned to a clear delimiting of the space—not just by the window surfaces themselves but also by a geometrically articulated façade that encloses the interior. There is also the effect of reflections in the panes: of the surrounding building or, from the interior, visitors and parts of the exhibitions. These often-charming reflections lead to perceiving the space not as a continuum but as clearly separated inside and outside worlds.[10] No one has brought out the way the panes form boundaries more clearly than the artist Imi Knoebel, who followed a spontaneous impulse to paint the glass walls with white distemper and thus illustrate the inherent sculptural value of the interior (fig. 5). The density and large volume of the hall suddenly became physically palpable, almost graspable. Space could be experienced as an artistic dimension, as "created" space.[11] Above all, however, this impressive intervention revealed how much this space is framed formally and aesthetically. The windows, Knoebel made clear, are far more than a delicate membrane. They number among the strong "defining" conditions of this space. They separate not only different climate zones from one another but also form a clear threshold between a museum world and an outside world.[12]

The noble fittings of the hall reinforce these differences between outside and inside. Cloakrooms of brown oak, marble-clad ventilation shafts, and polished granite flooring (inside) stand for an exclusive "art space" emphatically removed from the quotidian. The elimination of all boundaries between life and art that the artists of Pop and Fluxus advocated so passionately in the 1960s was never the intention of this building. It is not a timeless space, as is occasionally asserted, but a historically charged one. Rudolf Stingel illustrated this using the example of another impressive installation. The New York–based artist had a gray wall-to-wall carpet installed in the hall in 2010. Its curving Indian ornament (among other things) directed the eye to the materials: to colors and structures of the natural materials used as well as to the delicate, reduced play of colors in the hall (fig. 6).[13] This space is in fact by no means neutral. The built-ins, which from today's perspective seem almost luxurious, along with the dark steel and the hard stone floor establish stances, also in relation to the way art or culture is experienced and perceived within it. Dignity and a certain coolness and distance waft around this space. It is a modern space but not a contemporary one.

Another, widespread misunderstanding lies in the idea that Mies created a spatial "void" in this building.[14] It is more accurate to say that his increasing effort to reduce all the architectural elements led to an undefined, almost "abstract" space. Many authors have recognized precisely that as Mies's strong striving for the universal, for "higher unity" (Mies). This idea of an ultimate, "pure" space, this search for a "higher truth" in architecture, was founded on the writings of Romano Guardini and Martin Heidegger, to whose ideas Mies van der Rohe was close.[15] It pays to look back here at the Barcelona Pavilion; its principle of the open spatial arrangement has become so famous in part because it did not have to fulfill any concrete function of specific purpose at the Barcelona International Exposition in 1929. There was nothing to exhibit in it. The only exhibit was the pavilion itself.[16] In her impressive book *Mies van der Rohe und Japan,* Inge Andritz therefore speaks of the Barcelona Pavilion as a

5 *Imi Knoebel: Zu Hilfe, zu Hilfe …* (Help, oh, help …) exhibition, Neue Nationalgalerie, 2009

6 *Rudolf Stingel LIVE* exhibition, Neue Nationalgalerie, 2010

"spatially framed void," comparing the open and contemplative qualities in Mies's work to classical Japanese architecture.[17] "In Japan, the secular residence is influenced by the Zen tradition. It represents concentration—both material and spiritual—and is also a place of contemplation. . . . The fundamental void elevates both the [Japanese] house and the 'status pavilion' in Barcelona out of the profane, filling them all with an almost sacred energy. This is grounded not primarily in being empty of but rather in being empty for something that is more essential than the material."[18] This spiritual charge of the "open" is without a doubt present in Mies's oeuvre. In contrast to the spatial vision of the pavilion, however, the working method and also the buildings of the late, "American" Mies are very clearly oriented toward the intended uses. Whether the Federal Center, Crown Hall, or Neue Nationalgalerie, these buildings do not lead to a "being empty." The aspects of openness laid out here are not ends in themselves or deliberately placed symbols like those of Daniel Libeskind and his famous "voids." Mies van der Rohe is also far removed from existentialist spaces like those that the playwright Samuel Beckett created in his theater of the absurd around 1960 or that the young Bruce Nauman demonstrated in his oppressive studio videos. In the glass hall of the Neue Nationalgalerie especially, Mies was not interested in a negative form that "speaks for itself," in a deliberate "keeping open," but rather in creating possibilities. The design collages that Mies made for very different architectural briefs in particular reveal how the open spaces of the buildings sketched were repeatedly occupied by works of art. Mies was very conscious of the aura of the fine arts, which themselves lay claim to space and can create and develop their own spaces. Mies also saw his own efforts toward beauty and "perfection" reflected in the possibilities of art. Even if Mies did not live to develop a specific vision for how the hall was to be used, its artistic weight and use were never in question.[19] And here, in its social, societal, and artistic use, this large, open space has proven its worth extraordinarily well. The diversity of the more than 5,000 events held here from 1968 to the present—from minimal artistic settings by way of exhibitions of all kinds, openings, and receptions to elaborate concerts and performances[20]—demonstrates this impressively. "The large hall . . . has repeatedly offered us opportunities for an entirely new, different, artistic experience of space," as Angela Schneider, the director of the institution for many years, summed up its effect.[21]

Even if the hall can be understood as a solitary building—and as the true international star—the idea of the open, flowing space continues in the basement. The (lower) stairway hall should be seen as a pendant to the exhibition hall, radically limited, with neither daylight nor transparency. In this purist setting, the two symmetrically arranged stairways necessarily seem more important. Rigorously articulated and optimally lit by natural light from above, they seem almost like autonomous sculptures. In fact, the stairway hall is once again both: a functional place and an exhibition space. From the outset, the plan had been to have a ticket counter here, but the outer walls and the open areas in the space are deliberately identified as places for art. The "immersive" motif of all the architecture, which begins when stepping onto the terrace and becomes much stronger upon entering the glass hall on the upper floor—that is, the sense of being, as a visitor, part of one entire large art space from the outset, of being surrounded by visual art from the very start—is continued on the lower floor. The way painting and sculpture collide with the banal activities of the foyer such as ticket sales was even more radical in a time that strictly distinguished between "art" and "nonart" than it seems from our perspective today (fig. 7). The very first presentations from the collection begin in the stairway hall. Striking occasions in this hall, such as the very controversial hanging of formerly official "state art" by Willi Sitte in 1992, were discussed across Germany. Seen in this way, the stairway hall should by no means be grasped as a neutral foyer or Miesian space, but rather as a museum sphere that is already heavily laden with the contents of the collection.

Whereas the stairway hall comes across as somewhat sober and "dry" as a result of its hard boundaries, the museum spaces open up in the direction of the sculpture garden in a spectacular way similar to that of the hall. Mies spoke of a single, connected "Large Exhibition Space,"[22] which was to be articulated solely by several freestanding (and entirely variable) wall partitions. In order to further underscore the openness of this architecture, the prepared wall partitions pointedly end a good distance from the ribbon windows and thus permit an almost panoramic view of the garden. The famous, often-described derivation of the open floor plan in Mies van der Rohe's work from the artistic compositions of the likes of Piet Mondrian and the De Stijl movement[23] is more than clear in the basement. The open wall partitions correspond to the rectangular abstractions of early "Classical Modernism," and in their geometry are visually reinforced especially by the strict square articulations of the modular ceiling. The path through this so-called Large Exhibition Space is never a straight line, is more meandering, with ever-new perspectives on other rooms and on the large outdoor space of the sculpture garden.

The garden itself is an exhibition space. For Mies van der Rohe, it was never an exit from the museum. On the contrary, the high dividing walls make the courtyard the ultimate site of retreat and contemplation: a *hortus conclusus*.[24] Interior and exterior complement each other here: the inside of the museum (the exhibitions, the art) attains its apparent natural counterpart (fig. 4, p. 207) thanks to a view through to the outside (of the garden, of nature). In Mies's thinking, the clear idea behind this is that not only architecture but also art is always related to a reality. Mies had also considered similar relationships for the administration as well. Here, too, the processes of working should remain visible for the viewers from the collection through transparent partitions.[25] This reveals once again the principle of open architecture: the exhibition space should be understood as merely a detail from a much larger continuum of a general living space.

This tight intermeshing of very different spheres of space and life characterizes the collages of Mies van der Rohe in particular. Glued-in views of nature or works of art dovetail with perspectivally constructed spatial ideas. They make it clear how much Mies was thinking—especially when it came to the Neue Nationalgalerie—in terms of hung "paintings" with "sculptures" placed between them—that is to say, in terms of wall and figure. The spatial effect of the floor for the collection today is indeed strongly marked by the placement of the walls, which in the collages "block" or

7 Beginning of the exhibition *Der geteilte Himmel* (Divided Heaven) in the stairway hall, 2011

8 Barnett Newman, *Who's Afraid of Red, Yellow, and Blue IV*, 1969–70, oil on canvas, 274 × 603 cm, Staatliche Museen zu Berlin, Nationalgalerie

direct the gaze. The ceiling wallwasher in particular ensure such a strong focus on the walls that the space between the walls often seems to be a barely defined "in-between space." The relatively dark wool carpet, which swallows most of the light, results in a striking difference in brightness between the bright surfaces of the walls and ceilings as compared to the floors, which visually and spatially recede considerably. Only after sculptures are placed there and lit individually do these inner areas derive their own strength and attention.

The experience of the shell of the building (during the recent renovation and the resulting changes to the spatial proportions) made something interesting especially clear: how much the basement was laid out horizontally by Mies. The impression of vastness results, on the one hand, from the actual size of the floor (which is often underestimated) but above all, on the other hand, from the extremely long axis of sight through the building. Curatorially speaking, the floor is a great challenge, because despite the many partitions no real spaces are formed, just compartments in the overall flowing space. Here, too, as in the hall, an immersive principle of the space applies that does not unmistakably begin anywhere and never clearly ends. This particular spatial layout is also one of the reasons why the large painting in the collection *Who's Afraid of Red, Yellow, and Blue IV* (1969–70) by Barnett Newman has such a powerful effect on the basement floor (fig. 8). First, of course, its radical reduction (the colors, the composition, the subject matter) conforms entirely to the stringent vocabulary and thinking of Mies. Above all, however, this late work by Newman, which is more than 6 meters wide, stands for a spiritually charged color space, its force field engaging the viewer. Newman was trying with this painting to trigger an immediate and specific "experience." The viewer was supposed to approach the painting as closely as possible in order to experience the sensation of a complete space: "Anyone standing in front of my paintings must feel the vertical domelike vaults encompass him [in order] to awaken an awareness of his being alive in the sensation of complete space."[26]

This emphatically immersive concept that Barnett Newman was pursuing with his painting at the end of his life, and in which space and time and aesthetic experience fall into place together, characterizes the building of the Neue Nationalgalerie on all levels. The spiritual dimension of the likes of Barnett Newman is related to the spiritualized "order" of Mies. For this very wide, maximally planar painting, Mies prepared the ideal conditions with broad, long walls and the horizontal orientation of the entire floor. Despite all the networking, despite all the openness, Mies van der Rohe created for the museum its own sphere of art that is decoupled from the outside world in which art (on the wall or in the room) can have a particularly autonomous and powerful effect. Unlike the white cube that would become so popular later in the 1960s and 1970s, here in Mies's building in particular the elaborate glass doors, the gray wool carpet, and the brownish-red floorboards that run through all of the rooms on the lower floor ensure "resonance" with a strong cultural and historical element that always attends the viewing of art.

The unique spatial experience of the Neue Nationalgalerie lies precisely not in its timelessness but rather in the experience of a North American "modernism." The spatial inventions of Chicago and Toronto that Mies van der Rohe brought together here in this building can still be clearly felt today. Not only the hall, the real icon, but also the other rooms of the museum are always both maximally open and yet clearly defined, highly charged in a universal and yet culturally specific way. The breadth and size of the hall and the ambition thus formulated will continue to challenge statements and interventions from future generations of artists. On both levels, the museum offers unique opportunities to engage with the diverse art of the twentieth century—precisely because it is itself so much a child of the twentieth century.

1 See Pao-Chi Chang and Alfred Swenson, "Experiencing Crown Hall: Mies and the 'Open Region,'" in *Mies van der Rohe: Crown Hall*, ed. Werner Blaser (Basel: Birkhäuser, 2001), pp. 6–25.

2 Werner Blaser, "Mies van der Rohe 70jährig," *Wohnen und Bauen* 10 (1956), p. 217.

3 The point of departure for the collage *Concert Hall* (1942) is a slightly revised view of the interior of a factory building: the Glenn L. Martin Aircraft Assembly Building near Baltimore by Albert Kahn. See Andreas Beitin, Wolf Eiermann, and Brigitte Franzen, ed., *Mies van der Rohe: Montage, Collage*, exh. cat. Ludwig Forum Aachen, Aachen, and Museum Georg Schäfer, Schweinfurt (London: Koenig Books, 2017), pp. 160–61. See also the essay by Claire Zimmerman in the present volume, pp. 137–43.

4 Ludwig Mies van der Rohe, "Museum for a Small City," *Architectural Forum* 78, no. 5 (May 1943), pp. 84–85. Reprinted in Fritz Neumeyer, *The Artless Word: Mies van der Rohe on the Building Art*, trans. Mark Jarzombek (Cambridge, MA: The MIT Press, 1991), p. 322.

5 See, for example, "Mies moved from the complex to the simple," in Phyllis Lambert, "Mies Immersion," in *Mies in America*, ed. Phyllis Lambert, exh. cat. Canadian Centre for Architecture, Montreal, and Whitney Museum of American Art, New York (New York: Harry N. Abrams, 2001), pp. 192–589, esp. p. 423. It should be noted for the chronology that the basic design for the Neue Nationalgalerie goes back to the design for the headquarters of the Bacardi company created between 1957 and 1960.

6 See Lambert, "Mies Immersion," in *Mies in America*.

7 The ticket counter in the glass hall was never built. Early exhibitions in the hall were often separated from the entrance by cords.

8 Ludwig Mies van der Rohe, "Museum for a Small City," in Neumeyer, *The Artless Word*, p. 322.

9 Mies van der Rohe in conversation with Georgia van der Rohe: "It is such a large hall . . . that of course it means great difficulties for the exhibiting of art. I am fully aware of that. But it has such potential that I simply cannot take those difficulties into account." From Georgia van der Rohe's 1979–80 film for Knoll Furniture and Zweites Deutsches Fernsehen, quoted in Franz Schulze and Edward Windhorst, *Mies van der Rohe: A Critical Biography*, rev. ed. (Chicago: University of Chicago Press, 2012), p. 357; or see Phyllis Lambert: "For Berlin, Mies talked of the exhibition hall as a theater, a stage requiring the freedom to create different scenery for different installations." Lambert, "Mies Immersion," in *Mies in America*, p. 497. On the inadequacies of the hall, of which Mies van der Rohe was well aware, see, for example, Bettina Vismann and Jürgen Mayer H, "Perspiration; or, The New Nationalgalerie between Cold Fronts," in *When Things Cast No Shadow*, ed. Adam Szymczyk and Elena Filipovic, exh. cat. 5. Berlin Biennale für Zeitgenössische Kunst (Zurich: JRP Ringier, 2008), pp. 78–98.

10 On this, see the detailed study by Yilmaz Dziewior, *Mies van der Rohe: Blick durch den Spiegel* (Cologne: Walther König, 2005), esp. pp. 79–84 and 141–42, and Lambert, "Mies Immersion," in *Mies in America*, p. 499.

11 See Eugen Blume and Udo Kittelmann, ed., *Imi Knoebel: Help, Oh Help*, trans. Allison Moseley, exh. cat. Neue Nationalgalerie, Berlin (Berlin: Hatje Cantz, 2019).

12 On this, see Martino Stierli's reflection on motifs of distance in the work of Mies van der Rohe: Martino Stierli, "Die Visualität des Raums und der Raum des Sehens: Zu Mies van der Rohes späten Fotocollagen," in Beitin et al., *Mies van der Rohe: Montage, Collage*, pp. 126–38.

13 See Joachim Jäger and Udo Kittelmann, ed., *Rudolf Stingel: Neue Nationalgalerie Berlin*, exh. cat. Neue Nationalgalerie, Berlin (Cologne: Walther König, 2010).

14 See, for example, Phyllis Lambert: "the space of the pavilion is defined as emptiness, a void between the great heavy roof and its podium," in Lambert, "Mies Immersion," in *Mies in America*, p. 497, and Peter Eisenman, "Mies and the Figuring of Absence," in Lambert, *Mies in America*, pp. 706–15, esp. p. 711.

15 See Fritz Neumeyer, "Architecture for the Search for Knowledge: The Double Way to Order," in Neumeyer, *The Artless Word*, pp. 195–236; see also the texts by Alexander Schwarz, Günter Figal, and Erich Garhammer, in *Mies und die Poesie der Architektur*, ed. Albert Kirchengast, Jörn Köppler, and Wita Noack (Berlin: Form + Zweck, 2020).

16 See Dietrich Neumann with David Caralt, *An Accidental Masterpiece: Mies van der Rohe's Barcelona Pavilion* (Basel: Birkhäuser, 2020).

17 Inge Adritz, *Mies van der Rohe und Japan* (Salzburg: Müry Salzmann, 2018).

18 Ibid., p. 99.

19 See Ludwig Mies van der Rohe, "Die Museumsarchitektur ist Dienerin einer Aufgabe, nicht Selbst-Zweck" (1960), quoted in Dziewior, *Mies van der Rohe: Blick durch den Spiegel*, p. 171.

20 See Joachim Jäger, in *Die Ausstellungen: Neue Nationalgalerie, 1968–2015*, ed. Constanze von Marlin and André Odier (Berlin: SMB, 2018). A complete documentation of the countless events at the Neue Nationalgalerie has yet to be written. See also Imke Woelk, "Der offene Raum: Der Gebrauchswert der Halle der Neuen Nationalgalerie in Berlin von Ludwig Mies van der Rohe" (PhD diss., Technische Universität Berlin, 2010).

21 Angela Schneider, "Ausstellungen," in *Neue Nationalgalerie Berlin* (Munich: Prestel, 1997), pp. 120–125, esp. p. 123.

22 Note on Mies's original plans for the "Galerie des 20. Jahrhunderts."

23 See Detlef Mertins, "Architectures of Becoming: Mies van der Rohe and the Avant-Garde," in *Mies in Berlin*, ed. Terence Riley and Barry Bergdoll, exh. cat. Museum of Modern Art (New York: MoMA, 2001), pp. 107–33; Franz Schulze and Edward Windhorst, "Europe out of the Ashes: 1918–26," in Schulze and Windhorst, *Mies van der Rohe: A Critical Biography*, pp. 56–92.

24 See Dziewior, *Mies van der Rohe: Blick durch den Spiegel*, p. 139.

25 See Britta Bommert, "Studien zum Raumverständnis bei Ludwig Mies van der Rohe und Walter Gropius" (PhD diss., Universität zu Köln, Cologne, 2013).

26 Barnett Newman, in "'Frontiers of Space': Interview with Dorothy Gees Seckler," in *Barnett Newman: Selected Writings and Interviews*, ed. John P. O'Neill (New York: Alfred A. Knopf, 1990), pp. 247–50, esp. p. 250. On the spatial concept of *Who's Afraid of Red, Yellow, and Blue IV*, see also Armin Zweite, ed., *Barnett Newman: Paintings, Sculptures, Works on Paper*, exh. cat. Kunstsammlung Nordrhein-Westfalen, Düsseldorf (Ostfildern-Ruit: Hatje Cantz, 1999), esp. pp. 149ff.

AUFZUG
ELEVATOR
KASSE
TICKETS
SAMMLUNG
COLLECTION

AUFZUG
COLLECTION

AUFZUG
ELEVATOR
KASSE
TICKETS
SAMMLUNG
COLLECTION

AUFZUG
ELEVATOR
KASSE
TICKETS
SAMMLUNG
COLLECTION

The Base

Terrace and Podium of the Neue Nationalgalerie

Claire Zimmerman

An aerial view of the Kulturforum, taken in 1978, shows three major buildings: the Philharmonie (its Chamber Music Hall not yet present), the Staatsbibliothek zu Berlin (Berlin State Library), and the Neue Nationalgalerie (New National Gallery) (fig. 6, p. 158). The empty stretch of no-man's-land near the Berlin Wall to the right, the stripe of the Landwehrkanal in the foreground, and the Tiergarten at the back encircle the Kulturforum, an island in Berlin's postwar urban landscape. Within this constrained precinct, the flat square of the Neue Nationalgalerie roof floats evocatively over a massive podium-terrace on which it casts its shadow. This imposition of one perfect square atop another presents a dramatic contrast to the irregular prismatic assemblages of its two neighbors. From this view, the Neue Nationalgalerie is flattened—it is all terrace and roof—like a pair of blank slates laid down on the recently ruined city, awaiting the inscriptions of time. The roof is clearly defined; the square ground on which it stands, however, changes as one's eye moves across the site—continuous with the street at the front, yet demarcated by a sharp edge at the back, where the ground falls away into the cut of a garden courtyard. An open streetside terrace at the front becomes a podium at the back; two different agents inhabiting the same constructed object.

Terrace

The Neue Nationalgalerie commonly elicits comparison to Karl Friedrich Schinkel's work, and architecturally informed visitors (whether physical or virtual) are cued to draw the connection back to Ludwig Mies van der Rohe's Berlin predecessor.[1] Grounding the architect's final project in earlier buildings, Fritz Neumeyer argued for the wide stone terrace as an "urban counterpart" to earlier experiments in which open spatial zones offered staging areas *for thought itself,* setting the buildings contained within them into a distinctly separate frame. In a building such as the Farnsworth House, the architect cleared space, then filled it with construction that connected to its immediate surroundings while simultaneously standing apart from them; the Seagram Building and other urban campuses do the same. Neumeyer links this strategy to Mies's deep engagement with philosophers, showing how the architect thereby *constructed philosophy* in tangible material form. The terrace of the Neue Nationalgalerie does this both under the cover of its monumental roof, but also beyond: clearing a space in the war-torn city, enlisting the St. Matthäus-Kirche next door to define the edge of a precinct inside the larger precinct of the Kulturforum, staffing it with a glass pavilion and large-scale sculpture.[2] One is both inside the city and outside it, "like a clearing in the forest," as Phyllis Lambert eloquently describes this place.[3]

Others refer to the terrace as an "urban stage" on which performance unfolds, or as an "event space."[4] Yet the action that takes place outside and beyond the building, to which it serves witness, also makes the terrace a massive viewing platform for the city as work of art. A precinct separated from but continuous with the world around is indeed both stage and viewpoint. Anchored by its sculpture, the terrace pulls the exhibition space beyond the museum's weatherwall of glass. Extending the gallery space out into the city, it also constitutes the city as the subject of art. Visitors can look out upon its drama in all directions. When constructed, there was not much going on around the Neue Nationalgalerie—in the 1960s and 1970s, this was a quiet part of Berlin, but only recently so, and not for long. Its former liveliness as a cultural center suggests that the Neue Nationalgalerie viewing terrace was meant to be temporally inhabited as well: one looks out, after all, on a site with an extraordinarily difficult history.

Aerial photographs of the Kulturforum from the 1970s recall that history by showing its proximity to sites of recent cataclysm.[5] Mies's destroyed Am Karlsbad office, merely a stone's throw from the new building site on the other side of the Landwehrkanal, was demolished well before 1945. It was not only the Allied aerial bombing and invasion that damaged this part of Berlin, but also its location in the path of the gargantuan North–South Axis carved out in service of the vision pursued by the National Socialist architect and planner Albert Speer and by Adolf Hitler. The grandiose capital complex "Germania" was to turn Berlin into the imperial center of the Third Reich; the land on which the future Kulturforum would be built lay right in its path.

Mies's home and office lay in the construction zone for a 120 meter boulevard that constituted the main artery of Germania; the building had been razed by 1942, and Am Karlsbad wiped from the map. The catastrophe of Allied bombing thus was piled on the earlier catastrophe of Nazi urban planning. As the war advanced, plans for Germania were mothballed, as Germany turned all its efforts to war supply. The ruined hulk of Theodor Dierksmeier's tentacular Haus des Fremdenverkehrs (House of Tourism, constructed in 1938) on the massive Runder Platz, roughly where the current Staatsbibliothek zu Berlin – Haus Potsdamer Strasse by Hans Scharoun lies, remained on the site until 1963, as the Philharmonie went up nearby. The Neue Nationalgalerie terrace thus looks out on a battleground of history, literally and figuratively. That Mies himself chose the site during his 1961 visit to Berlin—the first since his 1938 emigration—suggests his awareness of this difficult history; he will have surveyed the ruins of the Haus des Fremdenverkehrs, behind which the future museum's terrace lay.[6] A 1961–62 panorama shows the empty site between the St. Matthäus-Kirche, the ruin, and the Landwehrkanal—an invitation to build (fig. 1). What might the seventy-five-year-old architect have thought as he surveyed the ruins of his former neighborhood?

Podium

The terrace of the Neue Nationalgalerie conceals its packed half-subterranean programmed spaces, at least from the street side. A terrace barely lifted up along Potsdamer Strasse becomes a podium—a raised platform containing space—from the garden side (fig. 2). Visitors to the exterior are unaware of this transformation until they reach the western edge of the terrace, where views into the sculpture courtyard below suggest that something is taking place beneath their feet. Why are so many of the museum's functions hidden underground? Where the terrace seems to belong to the city of Schinkel and German history, the podium has a darker genealogy that commemorates what happened to Mies after he left Berlin in 1937 for Chicago. This building, more than any other of his career, allowed "weav[ing] together . . . the threads of his German and American work," so that past and present influences are recast throughout.[7]

Mies's adopted country brought newfound industrial capacity to bear on the production of armaments and machines for the Second World War, straight from the industrial zones that surrounded Chicago, where he lived. The Allies turned the tide of the war on the eastern and western fronts by the winter of 1942–43, in part because Soviet rapid industrialization had transformed a giant agrarian nation into an incipient superpower, with a substantial infusion of American (and some European) technology driving Stalin's first Five-Year Plan (1928–32). The Stalingrad Tractor Factory, for example, would industrialize Soviet agriculture *and* tank production; by the end of the pivotal Battle of Stalingrad, the factory, designed and built by a Detroit-based architecture firm, was used as a defensive installation by Russian and then German soldiers. As for the United States, it was widely acknowledged that the seemingly impossible had happened: a country unfit for adequate war production as late as 1937 had established an unprecedented military infrastructure by 1942.[8] Albert Kahn Inc., architects of the Stalingrad factory, provided one of the largest plants in the world in the massive Dodge Chicago Plant built in 1942–43.

Given the industrial growth unfolding in the Midwest throughout the late 1930s and early 1940s, there is another precedent for the Neue Nationalgalerie podium besides that claimed for Schinkel's subterranean spaces.[9] Mies had been impressed by an interior photograph of Kahn Inc.'s 1937 Glenn L. Martin airplane assembly plant in coastal Maryland (fig. 3), which he and his student Paul Campagna used for the Concert Hall collage on which they initially collaborated in 1942 (fig. 1, p. 102).[10] A new typology for the large-scale airplane manufacturing facility had subsequently emerged at Glenn L. Martin's next two giant bomber factories, twin buildings on the Maryland campus and out in Omaha, Nebraska, both in 1941: keep the manufacturing floor entirely clear for the free movement of large aircraft, and pack program—entry, storage, canteen, locker rooms, lavatories, and meeting rooms—underneath.[11] At Plant #2 in Middle River, Maryland, the grade changes on site allowed densely programmed

1 Otto Borutta, one-hundred-degree panorama of the Kulturforum, including the Philharmonie, St. Matthäus church, and the ruined Haus des Fremdenverkehrs, 1961–62

2 Otto Borutta, aerial photograph of the Neue Nationalgalerie, 1968

3 Albert Kahn Associates, Glenn L. Martin Assembly Building (Plant #1), Middle River, Maryland, interior view, 1937

lower floors to be accessed and lit naturally from ground level, while new planes could roll directly out of the hangar onto the runway on the other side of the site.[12] This innovation in factory design was published in *Architectural Forum* in November 1941, where Mies or members of his office would likely have seen it (fig. 4). These planes were the very sorts of machines that hammered wartime Germany from the air, a bombardment about which Mies was known to have said that it "has to be done."[13] Using a similar spatial distribution twenty years later (and in the years between), Mies packed program into the Neue Nationalgalerie podium, creating the same radical contrast between dense programmed use below and a vast open yet enclosed space above.[14] A memorial to past history indeed.

Mies's encounter with Kahn's work is well known and dates to the late 1930s or early 1940s.[15] The 1942 Concert Hall project, collaged on top of a photograph of the 1937 Glenn L. Martin Plant #1 addition, indicates a curiosity about and interest in Kahn's work, but it also shows that Mies was testing out a practical use for enormous high-volume munitions buildings after the war.[16] The interior of the later Convention Hall design (fig. 6), cogently analyzed by Neil Levine and Martino Stierli, features a diminutive American flag collaged onto the composition.[17] Surely a tongue-in-cheek gesture to American patriotism, it may not have been Mies's. Interior photographs of aircraft manufacturing facilities, including but not limited to Kahn-designed buildings, show the same: American flags hanging from the trusses at multiple sites (fig. 5).

Turning back to Berlin, Kahn's work inhabits the podium of the Neue Nationalgalerie like a ghost. The reference is subdued, however, in uneasy tension with Schinkelesque neoclassicism through the ancient motif of the podium that reconciles irregular topography and regular construction, and the enclosed garden at the back—where the wide-ranging, extensive space of the terrace above is constrained and bounded for a different kind of meditation.[18] Was Mies ambivalent about war in 1942, when he composed the Concert Hall collage? Undoubtedly so, as a necessary evil that was urgently required to rid the world of fascist domination. Yet nearly twenty years later, when Dwight D. Eisenhower, in his fare-

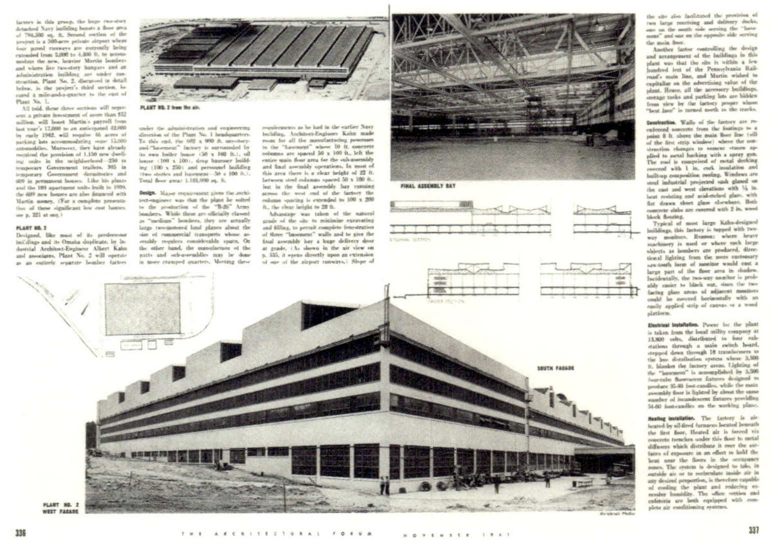

4 Glenn L. Martin Plant #2, Middle River, Maryland, illustration from *Architectural Forum* (November 1941)

5 Assembly building of Northrop Corporation, Hawthorne, California, 1944

6 Ludwig Mies van der Rohe, Convention Hall project, collage, 1953

well address to the American people, warned of the undue influence of the already robust US military-industrial complex in the midst of the escalating Cold War in January 1961, the world looked fundamentally different.[19] Two months later, Mies traveled to Berlin to pick his building site.

Conceived during the First World War, grown up during the Second World War, regnant in the postwar decades, and gone rogue since, the US militarized industry troubled architects throughout the postwar decades. Indisputably a part of the built environment, munitions plants and bomber factories were certainly *not* the architect's ideal program. Such programs reveal fundamental dilemmas of architecture since the Renaissance: that insalubrious political events can offer commissions large in size and generous of budget; and that architects have little ability to control the politics of the clients who commission them. Yet few reflected as cogently as did Mies on the presence of a new typology of giant military-industrial buildings, by 1963 one of which he had been aware for at least two decades.

The aerial bombardment of Berlin and of the former residential area around the Kulturforum resonates in this radical expansion of an architectural precedent. The source model is simultaneously disarmed and yet reinscribed in culture by its transformation into an art museum, the cultural playground of the same wealthy industrialists and state politicians who construct military might. Perhaps Kahn's hyperfunctional gigantic architecture was, if anything, the perfect mirror image to the giantism of Germania; Mies's museum, modestly scaled in comparison to both, offered a different alternative for building monumentally.

By the time the Neue Nationalgalerie was complete, Mies had lived a long life—almost exactly coincident with the maturation of industrialized war. His final built legacy echoed much of his earlier work: it reflected eloquently on conditions of architecture and urbanism in its present, certainly, but also on social organization and political history more generally. Far from occluding the military-industrial reality of the twentieth century, Mies's final museum design, like the earlier Concert Hall exercise, highlighted its operations by transmuting them into a site of human collective endeavor and public life.[20] The broad terrace above encourages contemplation amongst a collectivity. The busily industrious podium below allows focused concentration on works of art, provides space for curatorial-administrative tasks, and takes care of basic human needs. And yet together these two are one entity, separated by the thinness of a ceiling plane. The drama of this conjuncture—strains of Schinkel (local history) and Kahn (universal technology) reinterpreted by a humanist architect making sense of his own time by shaping public experience—ought not to escape us. People return to Mies's buildings again and again because they amplify history, not because they occlude it. They recall the time in which they were designed and, ideally, built. To see this architecture as "timeless" would be a mistake. It is precisely their sensitivity to time that makes Mies's buildings worth visiting again and again—and again in 2021, as a new world order replaces the one Mies knew, for better or worse.

1 Fritz Neumeyer, and Wolf Tegethoff have described a genealogy from Schinkel to Mies; on this, see Fritz Neumeyer, pp. 33–43, as well as the text by Wolf Tegethoff, pp. 80–89, both in the present volume. Philip Johnson linked the two architects in a speech of 1960, "Schinkel and Mies," published in *Schriftenreihe des Architekten- und Ingenieurvereins zu Berlin* XIII (1961), p. 24; reprinted in Philip Johnson, *Writings* (New York: Oxford University Press, 1979), pp. 164–81.

2 Fritz Neumeyer, *The Artless Word: Mies van der Rohe on the Building Art*, trans. Mark Jarzombek (Cambridge, MA: The MIT Press, 1991), p. 235. See also Fritz Neumeyer, "Space for Reflection: Block versus Pavilion," in *Ludwig Mies van der Rohe: Critical Essays*, ed. Franz Schulze (New York: MoMA, 1989), pp. 148–71.

3 Phyllis Lambert, "Mies Immersion," in *Mies in America*, exh. cat. Canadian Centre for Architecture, Montreal, and Whitney Museum, New York (New York: Harry N. Abrams, 2001), pp. 192–589, esp. p. 499; see also p. 17 in this volume.

4 Mark Jarzombek, "Mies van der Rohe's New National Gallery and the Problem of Context," *Assemblage: A Critical Journal of Architecture and Design Culture* 2 (February 1987), pp. 32–43; Detlef Mertins, "Mies's Event Space," *Grey Room* 20 (Summer 2005), pp. 60–73.

5 For a detailed discussion of the Kulturforum, see Christoph Hardebusch, "Culture Forum," in *Mies van der Rohe's New National Gallery in Berlin*, ed. Gabriela Wachter (Berlin: vice versa, 1995), pp. 32–55.

6 For Mies's selection of the site, see Sandra Honey, "The Office of Mies van der Rohe in America," *UIA: International Architect* 3 (1984), p. 50; also cited in Sonja Hildebrand, "Design and Construction of the New National Gallery," in Wachter, *Mies van der Rohe's New National Gallery in Berlin*, pp. 6–31, esp. p. 11, note 8.

7 Jean-Louis Cohen, *Mies van der Rohe*, 3rd and updated edition (Basel et al.: Birkhäuser, 2018), p. 160.

8 First through the Lend-Lease program, and later through direct participation in the war. Supplies to Britain began arriving as early as November 1939, in response to Winston Churchill's urgent pleas and despite robust resistance in the form of existing Neutrality Acts and from "America First" Nazi sympathizers such as Charles Lindbergh.

9 Wolf Tegethoff, "Die Neue Nationalgalerie im Werk Mies van der Rohes und im

Kontext der Berliner Museumsarchitektur," in *Berlins Museen: Geschichte und Zukunft*, ed. Christoph Hölz and Ulrike Steiner (Munich et al.: Deutscher Kunstverlag, 1994), pp. 281–92.

10 The source of transmission was George Nelson, *Industrial Architecture of Albert Kahn, Inc.* (New York: Architectural Book Pub. Co., 1938). See Cohen, *Mies van der Rohe*, p. 102; Claire Zimmerman, "New National Gallery," in *Mies in Berlin*, ed. Barry Bergdoll and Terence Riley (New York: MoMA, 2001), p. 358.

11 "Building for Defense," *Architectural Forum* 75 (November 1941), pp. 330–37; "Getting Ready for Bigger Airplanes," *Engineering News-Record* 119 (December 9, 1937), p. 941. Albert Kahn Associated Architects and Engineers, Inc., "Airplane Engines," *Factory Management and Maintenance* 100, no. 4 (April 1942), pp. B56–58. It seems that the packing of heating and utility lines under the 1937 building led to the next innovation: include human-occupied spaces in the podium. The same schema is used today at gigantic plants like that of Boeing in Everett, Washington.

12 Kahn subsequently used this spatial distribution frequently, for Glenn L. Martin, Curtiss Wright, the Chrysler Corporation, and Pratt & Whitney, among others.

13 For Mies's opinion on the bombardment of Germany, see Neil Levine, "'The Significance of Facts': Mies's Collages Up Close and Personal," *Assemblage* 37 (1998), pp. 70–101, esp. p. 99, note 46.

14 This is not to deny that references to Schinkel's Orianda Palace and even to the Altes Museum in Berlin may also be present; they are, however, less striking as direct parallels. But the history of art and architecture is not a zero-sum game, and Mies was evidently concerned with producing a "classic" solution that drew on both past and present. For these parallels, and a comprehensive contextualization of the Neue Nationalgalerie in the previous work of Mies, see Tegethoff, "Die Neue Nationalgalerie im Werk Mies van der Rohes und im Kontext der Berliner Museumsarchitektur," pp. 281–92.

15 Levine, "'The Significance of Facts': Mies's Collages Up Close and Personal," pp. 98–99, note 44. Note that Mies's own use of this program organization dates to Crown Hall (1950–56) and was used at the unbuilt Bacardi headquarters building in Santiago, Cuba, as well as the unbuilt museum in Schweinfurt. It reappears in bank buildings such as the Toronto-Dominion Centre, where it accommodates safety vaults and safes. The 1942 Concert Hall scheme, as Levine makes clear, was originally developed in collaboration between Mies and his student Paul Campagna.

16 Whether intentionally or not, Mies and Campagna selected the least typical building from among the Kahn firm's massive output for their Concert Hall scheme. The Glenn L. Martin plant in Middle River, Maryland, may be the exception that proves the rule. Built with a 91 meter clear span for planes that still spanned less than 60 meters wing to wing, the building was not purpose built to strict functional needs, as many Kahn buildings were. This one was a collaboration between architect and client for the sake of a bold experiment in clear-span building. They did it because they could, redirecting bridge trusses to the construction of a huge clear-span interior. I continue to think of Mies's scheme as one with practical ramifications.

17 Levine, "'The Significance of Facts': Mies's Collages Up Close and Personal," pp. 73–77; Martino Stierli, *Montage and the Metropolis: Architecture, Modernity, and the Representation of Space* (New Haven and London: Yale University Press, 2018), pp. 148–53.

18 On the Schinkelian genealogy of the podium, see Tegethoff, "Die Neue Nationalgalerie im Werk Mies van der Rohes und im Kontext der Berliner Museumsarchitektur."

19 See Dwight D. Eisenhower, "Farewell Radio and Television Address to the American People," January 17, 1961, https://www.eisenhowerlibrary.gov/sites/default/files/file/farewell_address.pdf.

20 Levine, "'The Significance of Facts': Mies's Collages up Close and Personal," p. 90. Also see Stefan Waezoldt's 1971 statement about the purpose of the museum as a potentially democratic public space, cited in Tegethoff, "Die Neue Nationalgalerie im Werk Mies van der Rohes und im Kontext der Berliner Museumsarchitektur," and Mertins, "Mies's Event Space."

The Garden

Barry Bergdoll

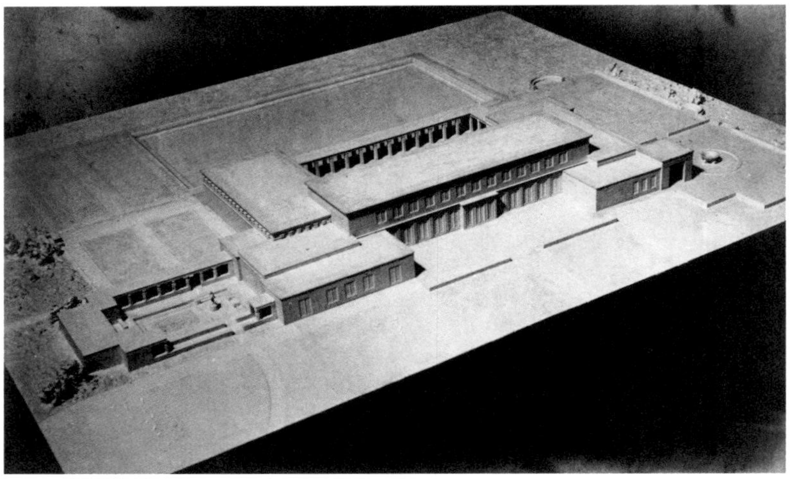

1 Ludwig Mies van der Rohe, Kröller-Müller House, Wassenaar, Netherlands, architectural model, 1912

A walled sculpture garden was the most significant addition that Ludwig Mies van der Rohe made to his unrealized project for Museum Georg Schäfer in Schweinfurt (1960–62), as he reimagined that design for West Berlin's emerging Kulturforum (fig. 2). For Schweinfurt, tall free-standing walls were to form a protective L-shaped enclosure around two sides of a glass pavilion set atop a podium (fig. 2, p. 164). These walls fell away in Berlin and the great glazed pavilion now stood freely, commanding city views in all directions, a veritable belvedere. The walls excised from the Schweinfurt model were, we might say, repurposed, lowered to form an extension of the podium itself. The result was not simply the addition of an outdoor gallery, but the crafting of a much more complex architectural section. With a continuous wall enclosing both solid and void, Mies created a composition balancing solid and void, a podium primarily solid but revealed to be void at its roofless western edge, a glazed void as universal gallery room under a monumental projecting roof balanced against the void of the sculpture garden visible only in aerial photography or as the final experience of a museum visit.

Mies's career came full circle with the open-ended invitation to build in postwar Berlin. Not only did he choose a museum of all the possible building commissions the Berlin Senate offered, but he selected Kemperplatz among the locations proposed, a site that had been literally in his view for the decades he lived and worked at Am Karlsbad 24 on the other side of the Landwehrkanal. The forms and technology of his architecture had changed dramatically in a quarter century in Chicago. Mies had developed methodically an architectural language of visible steel construction to craft an unprecedented liberation of space from structure. But he had never abandoned his fascination with integrating sculpture and nature in his architecture. This went back at least to his 1911 proposal for a house museum for the Kröller-Müller family at Wassenaar in the Netherlands, with its close integration of volumes of enclosed space and courtyards for planting and outdoor sculpture (fig. 1). In imagining a house for himself and his family in two bird's-eye sketches of an integrated residence and garden landscape at Werder, south of Potsdam, Mies affirmed his commitment to an approach to architecture in nature in which built rectangular

2 View of the sculpture garden of the Neue Nationalgalerie, 1968

3 Ludwig Mies van der Rohe, exhibition building at the *Deutsche Bauausstellung* (German Building Exhibition), Berlin, 1930–31

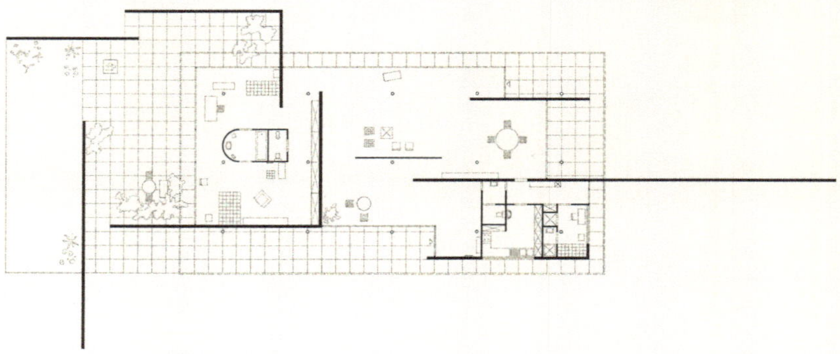

4 Ludwig Mies van der Rohe, floor plan of the exhibition building, 1930–31

volumes were placed into a taut relationship with outdoor rooms created by subtle shifts in ground plane. The open space around the house was structured not only by the building but by the architectonic handling of groves of trees. A single work of sculpture was carefully positioned at a key lynchpin. Long before he became the master of a new vocabulary for an architecture of steel and glass, of unbroken spaces and unprecedented transparencies, Mies had developed a syntax of abstracted architectural elements, natural vegetation, and figurative sculpture.

In the wake of his seminal design for the German Pavilion at the Barcelona International Exposition in 1929, Mies perfected a vision of architectural space—and of human experience of space—as a choreography of sliding walls in counterpoint to the guiding of the eye toward the horizon through the parallel planes of a gridded floor and a continuous ceiling plane. Roofless spaces formed of tall walls set at 90 degrees to one another were equally building blocks. But neither nature nor human form was evacuated from this new vision of spatial flow and expansion: carefully composed planting clusters and strategically placed figurative sculptures were integral to the design of the Barcelona Pavilion, as they would be to the typology of the Courthouse which dominated Mies's design work and teaching in the 1930s. This was brought home for exhibition visitors in Berlin in 1931 in Mies's Exhibition House for the *Berliner Bauausstellung* (figs. 3, 4), where the paved courtyard (unusual in its free-form masonry) juxtaposed potted trees with a life-sized statue of a female figure caught in mid-gait.

Mies's practice shifted dramatically in the United States, where institutional work quickly outpaced the residential design which had been the mainstay of his practice in Berlin. Invited to participate in the 1943 exercise of imagining all the components of an American postwar city, Mies rebuffed the invitation to design a church and proposed instead to design a museum. His Museum for a Small City (fig. 4, p. 37) is at once a manifesto on the role of the museum in postwar civic life and a transposition of much of his thinking in residential design, as well as the creation of a space for encountering works of art in the collective spaces of urban life. Syracuse, New York, was the city chosen by the editors of *Architectural Forum* magazine, who would publish the results in a special issue on the "New Buildings for 194x" (since no one could yet say when the postwar era would begin). But Mies designed for an ideal setting, a type that could be adapted to any American town—or German town for that matter—as a key component of the reconstruction of social, intellectual, and spiritual life after the war. "The first problem is to establish the museum as a center for the enjoyment, not the interment of art. In this project the barrier between the art work and the living community is erased by a garden approach which displays sculpture," Mies noted in a rare text accompanying one of his American designs. "The entire building is available for larger groups, encouraging a more representative use of the museum than is customary today, and creating a noble background for the civic and cultural life of the community."[1]

While sculpture gardens and the exhibition of sculpture in landscape settings became a leitmotif of the art scene after the Second World War—from the Henry Moore works set up in London's Battersea Park in 1948 to planning in the 1950s for the open-air sculpture garden of the Kröller-Müller Museum, opened in June 1961 in Otterlo, to designs by Henry van de Velde—Mies never pursued a separation of the dialogue between the space defined by architecture and the perception of the landscape and larger natural environment. "The interior sculptures enjoy an equal spatial freedom, because the open plan permits them to be seen against the surrounding hills. And what could be a more appropriate setting for sculpture than the landscape? The architectural space, thus achieved, becomes a defining rather than a confining space, and the effect of the room as a container is destroyed." For Mies, sculpture was not to be liberated by architecture, but maintained in a vital triangulation between architecture, art work, and nature.

Mies expanded the exercise assigned by *Architectural Forum* to cultural politics by making Picasso's *Guernica* (1937) a prominent feature of his design, noting that the monumental painting "has been difficult to place in the usual museum gallery. Here it could be placed to greatest advantage and become an element in space . . ."[2] Since the canvas had returned from a tour around the United States, Picasso's poignant cry against the German raid of the small Basque town of Guernica was to be housed in exile from Franco's Spain in New York's Museum of Modern Art. Its founding director Alfred H. Barr, encouraged by the founder of MoMA's Department of Architecture, Philip Johnson, hoped that the young museum, then in rented quarters, might entrust the design for a permanent building to Mies, whom Johnson considered the great architect of modernity. In 1939, the ten-year-old museum opened its new building by the architects Philip Goodwin and Edward Durell Stone on land donated by the Rockefeller family. A walled sculpture garden, visible from the floor-to-ceiling glass of the museum's ground floor vestibule and gallery, was an integral part of the design and conception of the museum from the first. Though the commission had escaped Mies, the architectural designs of the temporary garden that opened with the museum in 1939, as well as the complete redesign by Johnson in 1953, were nonetheless both deeply indebted to Mies's approach to space.[3] John McAndrew, Johnson's successor as head of MoMA's Department of Architecture (after Johnson was distanced from the museum by engagement in right-wing politics), created a first garden design, bounding the open area behind the museum on the north by a tall wattle garden wall, and inserting straight and half-circular free-standing spatial partitions—reminiscent of Mies's Tugendhat interior—as backdrops for the largely figurative sculpture. This was hardly an innovation, as Rodin had created a sculpture garden for his own work in Paris, which became an integral part of the Musée Rodin when it opened in 1919. And calls for museums to incorporate outdoor sculpture displays became commonplace in the 1920s. Still MoMA's sculpture garden was one of the first to conceive of the garden as a walled courtyard rather than a landscape garden or park.

In 1953, McAndrew's garden was razed to create a tabula rasa for a new garden with funds left in the will of one of the museum's founders, Abby Aldrich Rockefeller (fig. 5). Johnson, who had returned to the museum after the war and staged the first ever monographic show of Mies van der Rohe's architectural work,[4] created a powerful sculpture garden which revealed his close study of Mies's work of the previous decades. Swept away was the gravel floor of the garden in favor of a gridded pavement of striated gray marble; the vocabulary switched from garden to urban courtyard. As Peter Reed notes, "One of Johnson's primary design breakthroughs was the division of this 'roofless room' into four distinct asymmetrical areas for displaying sculpture. By means of steps, bridges, planting and pools Johnson subtly directs the visitor's circulation path. A pair of parallel reflecting pools, one 96 feet long and the other 50 feet long, slip past each other in a staggered arrangement."[5] Johnson proved himself here a fluent designer in a vocabulary established by Mies at the Barcelona Pavilion, noting even the design evolution of Mies's pavilion in which the reflective pool on the terrace shifted from being a symmetrical centerpiece of the outdoor space to a more dynamic element as it slid and locked into place bounded by two walls. Interestingly, the same evolution was recapitulated in Mies's design for the sculpture court at the Neue Nationalgalerie. Not only would the architecture of New York and Berlin's sculpture gardens evolve in dialogue—notably when Johnson added a raised eastern addition to the MoMA garden to allow an aerial view of it—but the curatorial approaches to display in the two sculpture courts had parallels. In each, the dialogue between geometric abstraction in the spatial layout, notably in crisp rectangular planes of water, was set off with a single dramatically placed figurative sculpture: a cast of Aristide Maillol's *The River* (1938) in New York, and Auguste Renoir's *Grande Baigneuse* (1917–18) in Berlin. The contrast between an ever-greater reduction of geometric spatial elements and figurative sculpture had become a leitmotif of Mies's architecture, reflected even in his approach to drawing plans, where the figurative sculpture was collaged onto the plan in elevation to emphasize the importance of the human figure as a counterpoint to abstracted architectural space.

The sculpture garden was no afterthought in Berlin. The initial brief had called for a place for open-air exhibition of sculpture, and Mies continued to rework the landscape and garden aspects of the design even as construction began. As Wolf Tegethoff has shown, a key change took place early in the design process, in 1963, when the idea of organizing the galleries within the podium assigned to show the permanent collection around a central courtyard, which

5 Abby Aldrich Rockefeller Sculpture Garden of the Museum of Modern Art, New York, 1953

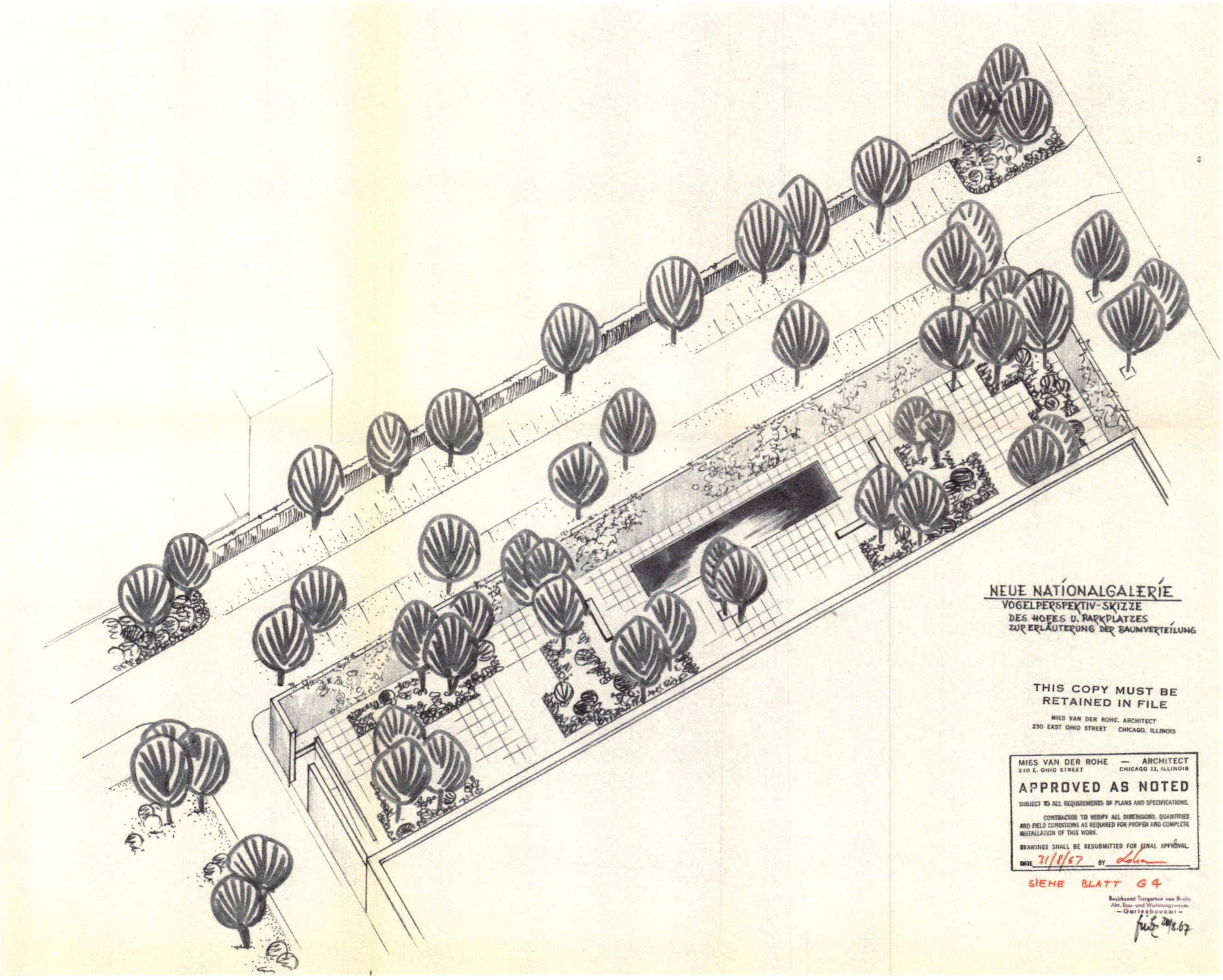

6 Ludwig Mies van der Rohe, sketch of the sculpture garden of the Neue Nationalgalerie, 1967

7 Heinrich-Siegfried Bormann, Ceph House, design of the courtyard house from Ludwig Mies van der Rohe's architecture course, 1933

served also as a source of natural light for the lower floor, was abandoned in favor of the sculpture garden as an appendage to the podium, outboard from the main gallery sequence as it were. In September 1963, Mies wrote to Werner Düttmann: "The museum garden doesn't seem half as favorable to me with the glass enclosing walls . . . I believe that the decision to be made here is an architectural one," defending the proposal for an annexed garden court. "Our proposal (for an adjoined garden courtyard) is clearer, more definite, is simply better architecturally."[6] Here the design went back to recapture the relationship between a roofless space bounded by uninterrupted walls—now of gray granite—which could be experienced prospectively as a stage set from the great glazed end wall of the galleries. For Mies this was preferable to a complex and confusing interplay of transparencies around a fully glazed courtyard. It was perhaps a carryover from the idea of the sculpture garden as a sunken atrium that the earliest plans, with the exteriorized sculpture court, featured a single large rectangular water basin centered in the space (fig. 6). As he had done over thirty years earlier in designing the podium of the Barcelona Pavilion, Mies worked his way toward a more dynamic composition of sliding and bypassing planes, a change that took place in the spring of 1965.[7] At the same time, the planting beds became more complex in form, not only in notched outlines but in the creation of small mounds of vegetation, whereby the garden was at once a landscape to stroll in and a panoramic landscape to be experienced from inside the galleries, much as Mies had staged the external world so strategically in projects from the Tugendhat House to the unrealized Resor House for the American Rockies, built around distant and close-up views of nature, to the Farnsworth House, where Mies professed: "If you view nature through the glass walls of the Farnsworth House, it gains a more profound significance than if viewed from outside. This way more is said about it—it becomes part of a larger whole."[8]

The design became ever subtler, not only in its geometric and botanic elements, but in relationship to the experience of viewing and entering this outdoor room seen both frontally from the lower vestibule of the museum and obliquely from the museum offices. Dirk Lohan, Mies's grandson, who worked closely on the design and served as liaison between Chicago and Berlin, made clear how Mies worked optically, often in large scale, even in a 1:5 mockup of the main exhibition hall of the future museum in the Chicago office.[9] Peter Carter, who worked in Mies's office in these years, attributed Mies's greater interest in specific plants, making his palette not simply one of geology but also of botany, as deriving from close collaboration in the 1950s with the American landscape designer Alfred Caldwell on various schemes, notably on Lafayette Park in Detroit.[10] Ever since the residential projects of the 1920s and 1930s (fig. 7), Mies cultivated a counterpoint between geometric architectural form, hanging and climbing plants projected for exterior walls, and the leafy sculptural masses of treetops. An explanatory memo accompanying Mies's final construction plans, dated March 10, 1967, underscores how integral the experience of nature was to the building in both its larger urban visage and in the more intimate setting of the sculpture garden. Groupings of trees were not to be understood in isolation, but as composing groups across space and through the transparent great hall. In the Galerie-Hof, as the sculpture garden is called in many documents, the botanical composition was even more precisely composed, from the ground cover of the mounds in the planters between the pavers—kept loose in gravel to allow occasional changes—to the groupings of trees. "Nine trees of different habitus are grouped in such a way that they effectively coalesce with the sculptures to be erected."[11] Adjustments to plants with attention to the microclimate of the court were proposed by the Gartenbauamt (Parks Department),[12] but the importance of nature to Mies's conception of architecture could not be clearer than his order to his secretary to type his entire June 1967 memo in capital letters: "I CANNOT RECALL ACCEPTING A CLIMBING WILD GRAPEVINE . . . I'D LIKE TO FURTHER EXPLORE THE IDEA OF OTHER CREEPERS," he insisted, noting that Lohan would study this with Herrn Fink of the Gartenbauamt on an upcoming Berlin visit.[13] No less was he willing to approve the tree planting scheme in front of the building on Potsdamer Strasse. "I'D LIKE TO VERY CAREFULLY SITUATE THE TREES IN FRONT OF THE BUILDING."[14] He promised to do this on his own next visit to the building site and insisted that before then the Great Hall be finished and all obstructions for viewing it be gone in time for him to compose directly on site the final relationship between the rhythms of nature and the panoramic views through the transparent architecture. Almost as though preparing for a concert, a final tuning of the plants was scheduled for August 26, 1968, three weeks before the dedication ceremony, in order to allow time to replace any specimens that had suffered from the dryness and heat that Berlin experienced in April of 1968. The final planting scheme evolved through continual back and forth between the Gartenbauamt of the Tiergarten District Office and Mies's office, in a comprehensive plan in which the plants in the sculpture court were an integral part of an overall landscaping approach for the site. In response to notes of conversations between Mies, Lohan, and the Tiergarten District Office, the number of trees in the Gartenhof was increased, even as the number of different species was reduced. Silver maples (*Silberahorn*) and Trees of Heaven (*Ailanthus glandulosa* or *Götterbaum*) were now to be preferred,[15] although adjustments were soon made in relationship to the availability of mature specimens in the municipal nursery as sugar maples (*Zuckerahorn*) took precedence over silver maples, and *Götterbaum* were replaced by honey locusts (*Gleditschien*), assuring a seasonal transformation of the landscape panorama in the sculpture garden.

The addition of a sculpture garden to the museum model first proposed for Schweinfurt brought with it an enrichment of the architecture as a theatrical presentation of city and of nature. The building now had two vastly contrasting levels, not only in the way art was displayed, but in the way the experience in the larger realm was framed. From the great glazed hall, with its display on view day and night to passersby, the changing speeds and scenes of the city could be surveyed from a 360-degree panoramic hall. Below, parts of the permanent galleries enjoyed a diorama of an exterior gallery that extended the interior realm into a tableau of plants, fountains, and sculpture. Mies's search for a continual dialogue between architecture, nature, and sculpture here reached its denouement.

1 Ludwig Mies van der Rohe, "Museum for a Small City," *Architectural Forum* 78, no. 5 (May 1943), pp. 84–85. Reprinted in Fritz Neumeyer, *The Artless Word: Mies van der Rohe on the Building Art*, trans. Mark Jarzombek (Cambridge, MA: The MIT Press, 1991), p. 322.

2 Ibid.

3 See Mirka Beneš, "A Modern Classic: The Abby Aldrich Rockefeller Sculpture Garden," in *Philip Johnson and the Museum of Modern Art*, ed. John Elderfield, vol. 6 of *Studies in Modern Art* (New York: The Museum of Modern Art, 1998), pp. 104–51.

4 Barry Bergdoll, "Walk in Collage: Mies van der Rohe's 1947 Exhibition at MoMA," in *Mies van der Rohe: Montage/Collage*, ed. Andreas Beitin, Wolf Eiermann, and Brigitte Franzen, exh. cat. Ludwig Forum Aachen (London: Koenig Books, 2017), pp. 172–87.

5 Peter Reed and Ann Temkin, "A Garden Grows," in *Oasis in the City: The Abby Aldrich Rockefeller Sculpture Garden at the Museum of Modern Art*, ed. Peter Reed and Romy Silver-Kohn (New York: The Museum of Modern Art, 2019), pp. 18–46, here p. 24.

6 Translated from the German: "Der Museumsgarten scheint mir nicht halb so gut mit den gläsernen Umfassungswänden . . . Ich glaube, die Entscheidung, die hier zu treffen ist, ist eine architektonische . . . Unser Vorschlag (für einen angegliederten Gartenhof) ist klarer, bestimmter, ist architektonisch einfach besser." Ludwig Mies van der Rohe to Werner Düttmann, September 13, 1963, Library of Congress, Washington, DC, Mies Archive, Box III, Folder 19, quoted by Wolf Tegethoff, "Die Neue Nationalgalerie im Werk Mies van der Rohes und im Kontext der Berliner Museumsarchitektur," in *Berlins Museen, Geschichte und Zukunft* (Berlin: Deutscher Kunstverlag, 1994), p. 291, note 19.

7 See "Protokoll," March 4, 1965, Ludwig Mies van der Rohe Archive, Museum of Modern Art, New York (hereafter MvdR Archive), Box 6.

8 Quoted in an interview with Ludwig Mies van der Rohe by Christian Norberg-Schulz, published in *Baukunst und Werkform* 11, no. 11 (1958), pp. 615–18. Translation cited from Neumeyer, *The Artless Word*, p. 339.

9 See Dirk Lohan, "Skizzen der Erinnerung: Zum 30jährigen Jubiläum der Neuen Nationalgalerie, Berlin," in *Neue Nationalgalerie Berlin: Dreißig Jahre*, ed. Paul Kahlfeldt and Andres Lepik (Berlin: Staatliche Museen zu Berlin, 1998), p. 9.

10 Peter Carter, *Mies van der Rohe at Work* (London: Phaidon, 1999), p. 121.

11 Translated from the German: "Neun Bäume mit unterschiedlichem Habitus sind so gruppiert, daß sie sich mit den aufzustellenden Plastiken wirkungsvoll verbinden." Bez. Amt Tiergarten von Berlin, Abt. Bau- und Wohnungswesen – Gartenbauamt, "Neue Nationalgalerie: Erläuterungsbericht zum Plan der gärtnerischen Anlagen," March 10, 1967, MvdR Archive, Box 6.

12 NGA Mitte (formerly Gartenbauamt Tiergarten), Aktenbestand Neue Nationalgalerie, NGA 6203-15-d, note from April 1967.

13 Mies had given up his idea of using roses on the walls in favor of wild wine, as roses would have required a trellis. Translated from the German: "ICH KANN MICH NICHT ERINNERN, EINE BERANKUNG MIT WILDEM WEIN AKZEPTIERT ZU HABEN . . . ICH MOECHTE DIE MOEGLICHKEIT VON ANDEREN KLETTERPFLANZEN WEITER UNTERSUCHEN." See "Bestandsplan der Gartenanlage nach Ausführung 1967/68," Gartenbauamt Tiergarten, March 4, 1969.

14 Translated from the German: "ICH MOECHTE DIE BAUEME VOR DEM BAU SEHR SORGFAETLIG PLACIEREN." Letter from Mies van der Rohe's office to Gartenbauamt Berlin-Tiergarten, June 13, 1967, MvdR Archive, Box 6.

15 Letter from Bezirksamt Tiergarten to Mies's office, August 21, 1967, MvdR Archive, Box 6.

8 View of the sculpture garden of the Neue Nationalgalerie, 1975

The Roof

Gridding Off the Sky

Manfredo di Robilant

From the standpoint of elements of architecture, it is difficult to grasp whether the roof of the Neue Nationalgalerie is also a ceiling, or vice versa. The two are so intertwined that they form a solid cover which divides the inner space from the sky, and their very fusion possibly embeds the most notorious formula of Ludwig Mies van der Rohe: less is more. Moreover, the Neue Nationalgalerie comprises two floors, but it is difficult to dispute that Mies individuated the climax in the cover, or that he conceived the whole building in order to give the illusion that the upper floor is a self-standing, independent, neat pavilion.

The cover of the Neue Nationalgalerie is 1.8 meters high, establishing a stunning ratio of nearly 1:5 with the 8.7 meters height of the covered space. The façades are 7.2 meters recessed from the edge of the cover, on each side: their transparency, combined with their shadowed position, makes them ancillary to the cover, in terms of architectural composition. The cover's massiveness is dramatized by a matte-black coat that contrasts with the light-gray stone of the podium. Gravity itself is visually challenged: colors make the high seem heavy, and the low seem light. Though the cover is not dull, because the edge beams are indented by the continuations of the seventeen beams which go in the opposite direction, with a regular rhythm of vertical lines distanced 3.6 meters apart. The output is a series of eighteen rectangles with a basis that is exactly double the height: an essentialized, steel version of a classical entablature. For all of these reasons, the cover of the Neue Nationalgalerie is so imposing that it possibly *constitutes* the building itself (ill. pp. 64–65). A comparison between two photos on the opposite page, taken from a similar standpoint, is particularly suggestive in this regard (ill. p. 155). The first was shot immediately after the cover was put in place; everything under it is still to be built. The second photo, taken from the finished building, reveals that this "everything" is barely noticeable. "Nearly nothing" under the cover might have been Mies's motto for the Neue Nationalgalerie, one of his last buildings, its monumentality prompted not by the scale, but rather by the cover's character: strong, impressive, geometric at first sight. The steel table generates the primary space under this cover; the façade, as a glass curtain, only separates the inner from the outer space. On the inside, the partitions do not touch the cover, so as to leave the ceiling as visible as possible from behind. Moreover, the beams would have been deformed very minimally due to temperature variations throughout the day and the year, which is why it was necessary to decouple the roof from the beams.

The highly diffused iconography of the Neue Nationalgalerie suggests a laical temple dedicated to a new Germany. The cover is the dominant element of this iconography, because it is much thicker than the columns. In this sense, the Neue Nationalgalerie is antinomic to the Walhalla, in Regensburg, conceived by Ludwig I of Bavaria in the early nineteenth century to celebrate the German past. The Walhalla closely follows the model of the classical Greek temple, and therefore it is first and foremost about its massive columns, which support a pediment and a roof (fig. 2). Conversely, in the Neue Nationalgalerie the columns are just two per side, and each is distanced 18 meters from the corner, giving it a surprising visual lightness. There is also another architectural opposition between the Neue Nationalgalerie and the Walhalla: the architect of the latter, Leo von Klenze, exploited the dramatic slope on which the building stands to show it in its wholeness. Mies, on the other hand, exploited the variance in height at the building site to conceal the basement (fig. 2, p. 139).

One of Mies's first projects was an unsuccessful submission to a competition, in 1910, for a memorial to chancellor Otto von Bismarck (fig. 3). In his proposal, the young architect responded to the brief with two wings of colonnades featuring columns that had a square plan and no capitals, surmounted by a nearly smooth entablature. The majestic rendering somehow suggests that the theme of the Neue Nationalgalerie cover was already in the chords of Mies, because the simplicity of the entablature visually emphasizes its horizontality: the columns are thick, but the ratio between vertical and horizontal lines in the composition starts to resemble the Neue Nationalgalerie.[1] The project for the Bismarck memorial seems like a prequel to Mies's lifelong fascination with the pavilion as the elected architectural typology for always pushing forward the boundary of his

1 Shell of the Neue Nationalgalerie, 1967,
and exhibition hall of the Neue Nationalgalerie, 2001

2 Leo von Klenze, Walhalla, Donaustauf, ca. 1843

3 Ludwig Mies van der Rohe, design for the Bismarck Monument, Bingen, 1910

less is more motto.[2] The typology of the pavilion implies a narrow relationship between roof and ceiling, but it is not obvious that they overlap; there are nuances, and Mies went through many of them during his oeuvre. In the Neue Nationalgalerie, he reached a climactic fusion between the two elements, making it the most radical achievement of his work as a "pavilionist."

The first built pavilion by Mies was designed with Lilly Reich to represent Germany at the Barcelona International Exposition in 1929. The lower surface and structure of the roof are completely concealed by a white-coated, smooth dropped ceiling that also plays the role of soffit, due to its overhangs. The same happens in the Farnsworth weekend house, close to Chicago, completed in 1951. In both cases, because of the limited dimensions of the pavilion, the beams do not need to be very thick, and thus the profile of the cover does not overwhelm the building below. In other cases, where the dimensions of the pavilion called for thick beams, Mies opted to break the smoothness of the cover's profile and to place the beams above it, so that the roof is hanging from them. One such example is Cullinan Hall, for the Houston Museum of Fine Arts, built in 1954 (fig. 5). The same happens in Crown Hall, on the campus of the Illinois Institute of Technology, Chicago, built in 1956 (fig. 1, p. 58). At a grand scale, the cover of the unbuilt Chicago Convention Hall, conceived in 1954, does the opposite: the structure is visible from below, with its dramatic, white truss beams that influence the composition of the façade[3] (fig. 4). In each of these three pavilions, the cover has no overhangs and thus creates no "open-but-covered spaces": it merely creates indoor space. Except in the Convention Hall project, in all of the buildings mentioned above, partitions from floor to ceiling prevent the cover from being viewed from below in its entirety. The possibility of this view was envisioned by Mies in two sketch projects of 1942: a project for a Concert Hall and one for a Museum for a Small City. In the first, portions of the indoor area are covered by flimsy ceilings dropped from the truss beams of the cover. The result is a partial interruption of the continuity of its vision (fig. 1, p. 102). Yet the second anticipates the Neue Nationalgalerie theme of a huge cover sustained by a few slender columns[4] (fig. 3, p. 82);

4 Ludwig Mies van der Rohe, model for the Convention Hall project, 1954

5 Ludwig Mies van der Rohe, Cullinan Hall, Museum of Fine Arts, Houston, Texas, 1974

6 Aerial photograph of the Kulturforum with the square roof plate of the Neue Nationalgalerie, 1978

in the drawings, the structural concept of the cover is mostly left to the imagination.

Conversely, in the Neue Nationalgalerie, Mies had to be very specific about the cover, of course, and this was meant to include structural thinking as well. It seems that he conceived the cover as a plan—or, better, as a perfectly balanced field of forces—that was generated by structural engineering calculus. The plan needed a third dimension, because—architecturally—it had to play the role of an entablature. The height of the edge beams was again defined by the calculus of the structural engineers.[5] The distance between the nineteen main beams for each direction—a figure that includes the edge beams—defined the "rhythm" of the cover's lateral composition. When it came to construction, which was carried out by the German company Krupp-Druckenmüller, the building method that was employed faithfully followed the design concept. The "lift slab" technique came into fashion in the US construction industry around the mid-1950s, so it was not unusual in 1965, when construction on the Neue Nationalgalerie started. In September of that year, Mies traveled to Berlin for the cornerstone ceremony, and two years later he visited again in order to assist in the completion of the hydraulic positioning of the cover. The presence of the architect for the celebration of this moment—which was also the last time he came to the site—testifies to how crucial he rated the cover for the Neue Nationalgalerie architecture. The construction process was inherently spectacular and garnered huge attention, though it was not experimental. The "lift slab" technique involved assembling a slab on the ground and then lifting it to the desired height, 8.70 meters in this case. The eight load-bearing columns were attached to the same hydraulic jacks that were used to lift it up, so that from a quasi-horizontal position they were brought into their final, vertical position (ill. pp. 50–51). After the columns were fixed to the ground (that coincides with the concrete slab of the lower-level ceiling), the cover was dropped from the circa 15 centimeters added to the final height of 8.70 meters and fixed to the heads of the columns. Usually, the process is the opposite—the cover is built on the columns—but in the case of the Neue Nationalgalerie, the crucial role of the cover in the architectural design was copied in the construction, something that is not obvious when a project is translated from drawings into a building, especially a complex one. In the case of the Neue Nationalgalerie, complexity was prompted by figures: the cover—in plan, a square—spanned more than 64 meters and weighed circa 1,200 tons overall (fig. 6). In order to keep the visual impression of perfect horizontality from below, the beams were given a preliminary upward pre-curve of about 2 percent of their length, because the human eye perceives a very long line above it as curving to the ground.[6] The connection with America is not only evident in the construction technique but is still very visible in the silky matte black of the Berlin pavilion cover, which characterized the majority of Mies's US buildings, and which created, in urban scaled projects such as the Federal Center in Chicago and the Toronto-Dominion Centre, the very consistency between pavilions and towers.

As to the indoor space of the pavilion, in the Neue Nationalgalerie partitions are detached from both the cover and the floor. From a utilitarian point of view, this detachment served to ensure flexibility; from the point of view of aesthetics, it allowed the visual continuity of the horizontal plans of floor and cover. In this regard, the temporary installation by David Chipperfield (2014) was a spectacular mise-en-scène that highlighted how the cover ought not to be touched by columns (fig. 7), because it was designed to appear from below as a huge floating surface.[7] In the Neue Nationalgalerie, everything is visible through the aluminum grids: the steel beams and the steel plate of the roof. The same is true for the soffits of the 18 meter overhangs. The Neue Nationalgalerie's cover is related to the daily life of the building, because it hosts the heating, air conditioning, and anti-fire systems, but they are hidden not by a dropped ceiling, but by the structural grid of the secondary structure, which measures 3.6 by 3.6 meters. The response to utilitarian needs overlaps with symbolical values, for instance aesthetics, that are defined by structure. Conversely, to make another comparison, in the entrance pavilion of the Chicago Federal Center, designed by Mies's office these same years, the systems are hidden by a dropped ceiling punctuated with lights that make it resemble a starry sky, therefore making the roof invisible from below (fig. 5, p. 196).

In conclusion, the Neue Nationalgalerie features characteristics that maximize the importance of the cover: it extends well beyond the façades (as in the Barcelona Pavilion and the Farnworth House, but with dramatically larger projection and on every side), it is wholly visible from below (as in the Museum for a Small City project, which was much smaller in scale), and it is silky matte black, therefore visually heavy (as in Chicago and Toronto, but with no towers compensating for the horizontality of the volume).

1 Mies's submission was shortlisted among forty others out of a total of 379, but it was set aside because of the high budget it required. Despite its affinity with Schinkel's neoclassicism, the proposal was consistent with the rejection of historicism that characterized the majority of the entries to the competition: Jean-Louis Cohen, *Ludwig Mies van der Rohe*, 2nd rev. ed. (Basel et al.: Birkhäuser, 2007), p. 18.

2 The motto was appropriated by Mies from a comment he had heard from Peter Behrens while Mies himself was a young practitioner in his office, working on the temple-like façade of the Fagus-Werk, Berlin. See Detlef Mertins, *Mies* (London and New York: Phaidon, 2014), pp. 36–37. Due to the fact that this was in 1908, it is arguable that Mies bore in mind these words in his submission for the memorial to Bismarck. In this case, the lifelong research conducted by Mies on pavilions would actually be born as a struggle for the essential: the Neue Nationalgalerie seems, in fact, to close a circle that Mies started to trace with the paper project of 1910.

3 Discussing the photomontage that soon became the most iconic representation of the project, Martino Stierli associates it with the Neue Nationalgalerie, because both are "generic" spaces. See Martino Stierli, *Montage and the Metropolis: Architecture, Modernity, and the Representation of Space* (New Haven and London: Yale University Press, 2018), p. 155.

4 "The columns virtually disappear under the floating roof . . ."; Cohen, *Ludwig Mies van der Rohe*, p. 101.

5 The entire process of calculus and construction of the Neue Nationalgalerie cover's steel structure was published by the engineers who were in charge: H. Oeter and H. Sontag, "Das Stahldach der Neuen Nationalgalerie in Berlin," *Der Stahlbau* 4 (April 1968), pp. 106–15. For an in-depth, visual analysis of the construction, see Edgar Stach, *Mies van der Rohe: Space, Material, Detail* (Basel: Birkhäuser, 2017), pp. 138–47.

6 The author thanks Prof. Eng. Vittorio Nascè for the precious conversation on the structural implications of this essay.

7 On the role of free-standing columns in Mies's architecture, see Marco Pogacnik, "The Art of the Noblest Ornaments: The Statue and the Column in the Architecture of Mies van der Rohe," *Architectura: Zeitschrift für Geschichte der Baukunst* 40, no. 1 (January 2010), pp. 21–54.

7 *David Chipperfield: Sticks and Stones* exhibition, 2014

The Grid

Measure and Order in the Architecture of the Neue Nationalgalerie

Constanze von Marlin

The grid is measure and order in architecture. It signifies organization, clarity, and economy in the sense of rationalization. At the beginning of the 1920s, Ludwig Mies van der Rohe was exploring the potential of new methods and materials in architecture. In addition to concrete, iron, and glass, this also included the dividing of spatial masses according to function, organizing the floor plan, and the resulting ordering of the façade.[1] Mies van der Rohe worked with different grid sizes in his buildings. They serve the function of organizing both the constructive structure of a building and the size of the space. He determined the "building module" individually based on the uses and size of the building. The grid for the Toronto-Dominion Centre (1963–69) measured 5 feet (ca. 1.5 meters); the Convention Hall (1953–54) in Chicago was planned based on a measurement of 30 feet (ca. 9 meters).[2]

In the presentation portfolio for the Neue Nationalgalerie from 1963, Ludwig Mies van der Rohe indicates a grid measuring 90 by 90 centimeters. Since the brief was to build a museum, this grid is a unit of measurement that was not subject to any standards that, for example, an office building would have to meet and could be chosen purely on an aesthetic basis. Over the course of the planning process, the square as the basic unit of measurement was increased to 120 centimeters.[3] It appears first with the granite slabs of the terrace, their length corresponding to the main grid of 120 centimeters.[4] Mies used this grid to define the entire basic structure of the building in order to achieve a coherence of planning combined with clarity of form within a design order. "The structural systems employed are in accordance with the requirements of the respective functions, and the components of these systems are revealed both internally and externally."[5] The result is a design that has a rhythm reflected in all its details, from its construction to its surfaces, while at the same time maximizing spatial freedom. The almost undivided space of the exhibition hall of 50.4 by 50.4 meters is spanned by a self-supporting roof of 64.8 by 64.8 meters. At the same time, the use of a grid system has one special feature in the case of the Neue Nationalgalerie: it defines not only a unit of length but also the form of the building's floor plan: a square (ill. p. 56).[6]

When Gene Summers, who was the chief architect at Mies van der Rohe's firm at the time, proposed a rectangular, two-story building modeled on Crown Hall at the Illinois Institute of Technology in Chicago for the museum in Berlin that had been commissioned by the Berlin Senate, the architect decided: "Forget it, we are going to do the Bacardi/Schäfer concept. That belongs to Berlin."[7] He was referring to the further development of an unrealized 1957 design for the square administration building of the Bacardi rum maker in Santiago de Cuba, which then in 1960 served as the basis for the planned Museum Georg Schäfer in Schweinfurt, which also remained unbuilt.

Since his design for the Fifty by Fifty Feet House of 1950–52, Mies had been developing houses with a square floor plan and a structure that now coincided perfectly with the grid of the base (fig. 1). When developing his buildings, he preferred this floor plan because it enabled him to convey immediately both the structural form and the spatial composition. On the site plan in his presentation portfolio for the Neue Nationalgalerie, the black square of the roof plate dominates on a grid of small squares. At first glance, the length of the edge of the terrace also seems to form a square on the irregular lot. This impression is deceptive, however, as is the apparently centered placement of the exhibition hall, which is indeed square. By means of minimal deviations from an arrangement calculated purely mathematically, Mies demonstrated how important the perceived impression of architecture always was, which is why he also trusted his trained eye more than an unconditional faith in the principle of a defined grid.[8] For the Barcelona Pavilion (1929), Mies was already using a floor plan whose grid provided orientation for the placement of the partitions but did not represent a set of rules to be followed strictly. The eight filigreed, chrome-plated steel supports bearing the reinforced-concrete roof form a pair of rows with four outermost supports that are located at the point of contact of four floor plates. The supports in between them, however, are mathematically closer together than the outer supports, which is due to a purely aesthetic decision by the architect. In 1927–28, he wrote in lecturer notes: "Any attempt to solve building art problems by calculating means must fail."[9]

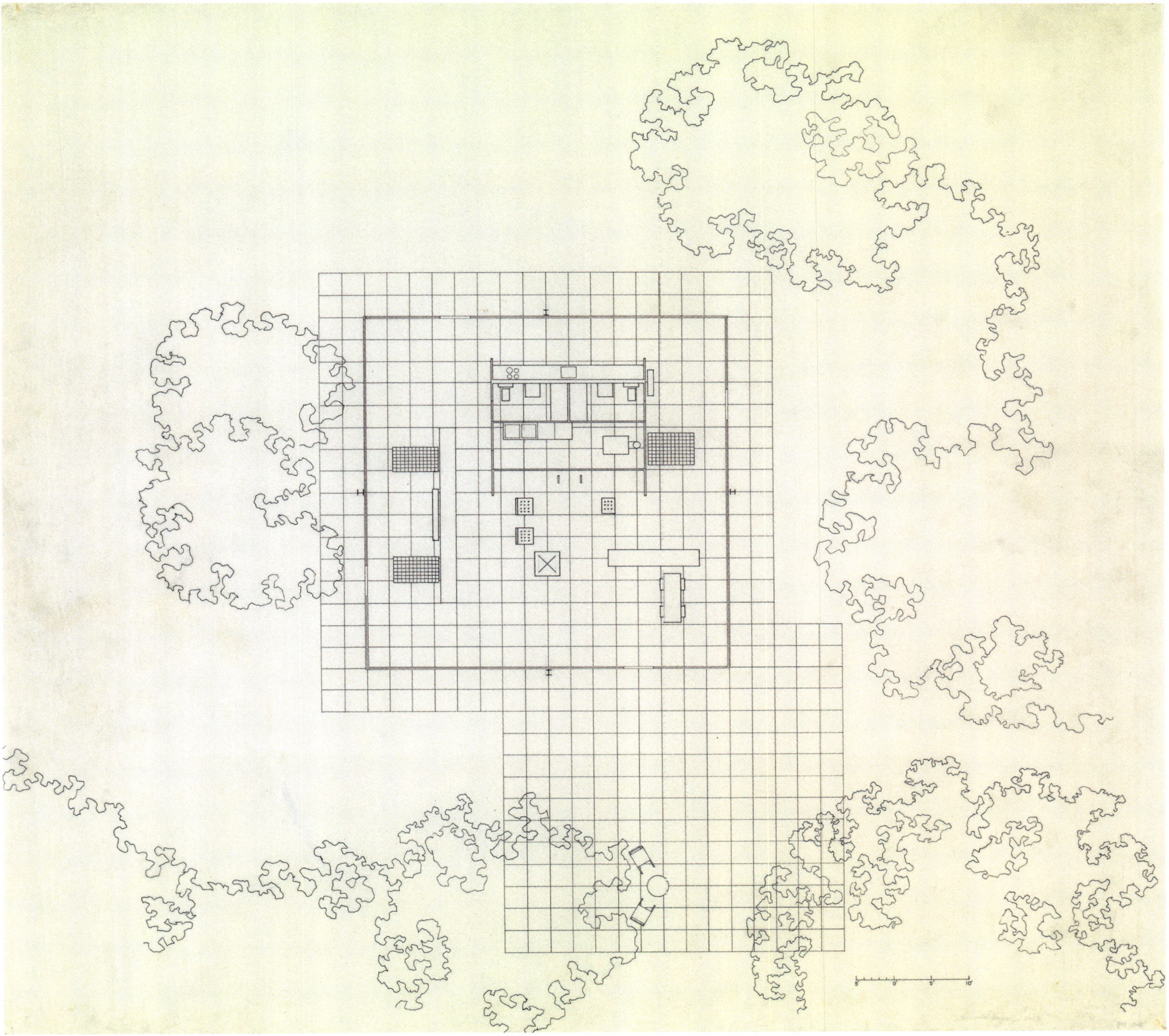

1 Ludwig Mies van der Rohe, Fifty by Fifty Feet House, floor plan, 1951–52

2 Ludwig Mies van der Rohe, architectural model of Museum Georg Schäfer, Schweinfurt, 1962

3 Ceiling and floor grids of the Neue Nationalgalerie, 2021

Mies used the grid not only to derive the measurements of the building but also to produce a visual impression. On the collages in the presentation portfolio of the Neue Nationalgalerie (fig. 4, p. 85), the square floor grid is aligned toward a central point in the center of the image. The ceiling, by contrast, is not defined further; the perspective shows it only as a blank plane. Apart from the real intention of the collage—demonstrating the presentation of art in the form of a suggestive visuality—this rendering conveys the idea of a spatial design that shows the grid as a design element for the furnishings, which is why no repetition of the ceiling was planned. Over the course of the planning process for the Neue Nationalgalerie, that arrangement was reversed. The floor of the rooms for the collection were given a uniformly gray carpet, and the ceilings were fitted with square modules.

As was usually the case with Mies's buildings, a suspended ceiling had originally been planned for the exhibition hall of the museum in Berlin (fig. 2). Considerations related to the presentation of paintings, however, ultimately led to the idea of hanging walls, which could not have been fastened to a suspended ceiling. The solution of leaving the roof construction exposed and inserting grilles into the square openings had not been used previously in Mies's work. This technical-aesthetic design element emphasized the room in its basic square form and gave it its characteristic look, including lamps in the coffers of the ceiling (fig. 3).

Although the grid is a stylistic element that represents the aesthetic of the museum building as a whole, it is not a concept that Mies van der Rohe would have chosen to describe his idea of architecture. In his inaugural speech at the Armour Institute of Technology in Chicago in 1938, the architect summed up his effort: "In its simplest form architecture is entirely rooted in practical considerations, but it can reach up through all degrees of value to the highest realm of spiritual existence, into the realm of the sensuously apprehendable, and into the sphere of pure art."[10] Striving for an unconditional aesthetic was therefore of utmost importance for his design practice. The square on which the order of the Neue Nationalgalerie is based is simple, absolute, universal, literal. By means of this geometric form, the architecture of the Neue Nationalgalerie emancipated itself from its function as a museum and extended itself into the artistic realm.

The square as the fundamental module of design—completely balanced and harboring no idiosyncratic surprises—also interested American Minimal artists in the 1960s because it offered a rational means of avoiding formal and subjective inventions. Establishing the length of just one side already defines the entire object. In its precision and neutrality, it represents a universal standard of a human-made form, a social form in the truest sense. Striving for a phenomenological presence of objects, the goal of the Minimal Art of the early 1960s was to design a literal and evident art whose objects were reduced to simple and clear, usually geometric, basic structures: "primary structures."[11] In 1968, the artist Tony Smith had the ultimate reduced object produced, *Die,* based on a model from 1962. He ordered by telephone "a six-foot cube of quarter-inch hot-rolled steel with diagonal internal bracing" from the Industrial Welding Company in Newark, New Jersey. With its edges about 180 centimeters long, the cube is too large to see over it; it can, however, be grasped with one glance, since every side is identical. Donald Judd often worked with simple geometric forms in a row. His *Untitled* (1976) from the Marx Collection is found in the Nationalgalerie (fig. 4). Its four polished, closed, stainless-steel cubes with edges 100 centimeters long are placed next to one another at regular intervals, close enough to be perceived as one work that includes the in-between space in the presentation.

It is not just in his striving for objectivity, clarity, and logic that Mies's ideas align with the approaches of Minimal Art, but also in his concept of space. Minimal Art's grappling with the real, both in terms of the material and of the form and presentation, influenced his understanding of space. No distinction between aesthetic and real space is made any longer. Because sculptural space is no longer marked by a pedestal, and hence is aesthetically transported away from real space, the presence of viewers becomes a component of the work of art. This idea of space assumes that space represents a condition of experience in which all perception—and, beyond that, all experience—is accompanied by space in that the perception of an external object is already spatial.

It is intentional that minimalist works of art should not be perceived by the eye alone but also by the body.

The physical experience of space plays an essential role in Mies's view of architecture as well. It is precisely in the openness of universal space and in the indeterminacy of Mies's concept of flowing space that the visitor is granted as much freedom to choose a path as possible. "Mies abandons the traditional principle of enclosed spaces and replaces it with a succession of spatial effects. The floor plan does not provide any insight with regard to boundaries; the walls are placed eccentrically ad infinitum."[12] In this view, building has a genuinely conceptual core, but also a political one: autonomous users with equal rights. In the first design for the exhibition hall in the presentation portfolio, the hierarchical division into a foyer and an exhibition space, which was supposed to be marked by a counter placed crosswise, has disappeared and been absorbed by the nonhierarchical unit of the square.

In the 1950s and 1960s, the nonhierarchical order of grid, module, and symmetry was being discussed not only in the fine arts but also in music. The compositional principles of John Cage are based on the idea of music as an aesthetic and social experience that has no finished form. Cage was searching for a way to translate indeterminacy into musical notation. For *Music for Carillon, #4, Page 3* (1961), notated dots on graph paper (fig. 5) that indicate musical parameters such as pitch on a temporal axis are freely interpreted by the musicians during the performance. If indeterminacy in music also included the unintended noises of the surroundings, then the glass architecture of Mies reflected precisely that openness, since "the glass houses of Mies van der Rohe reflect their environment, presenting to the eye images of clouds, trees, or grass, according to the situation."[13]

As early as 1929, Mies van der Rohe had the opportunity to separate the structural and spatial elements of architecture. In the German Pavilion at the Barcelona International Exposition, he implemented for the first time the idea of liberating walls from their load-bearing function and creating a fluid transition between inside and outside. Two design principles preoccupied him all his life: the free floor plan and flowing space. The grid served Mies as an organizational

4 Donald Judd, *Untitled*, 1976, polished stainless steel, four parts, each 100 × 100 × 100 cm, Staatliche Museen zu Berlin, Nationalgalerie, Sammlung Marx

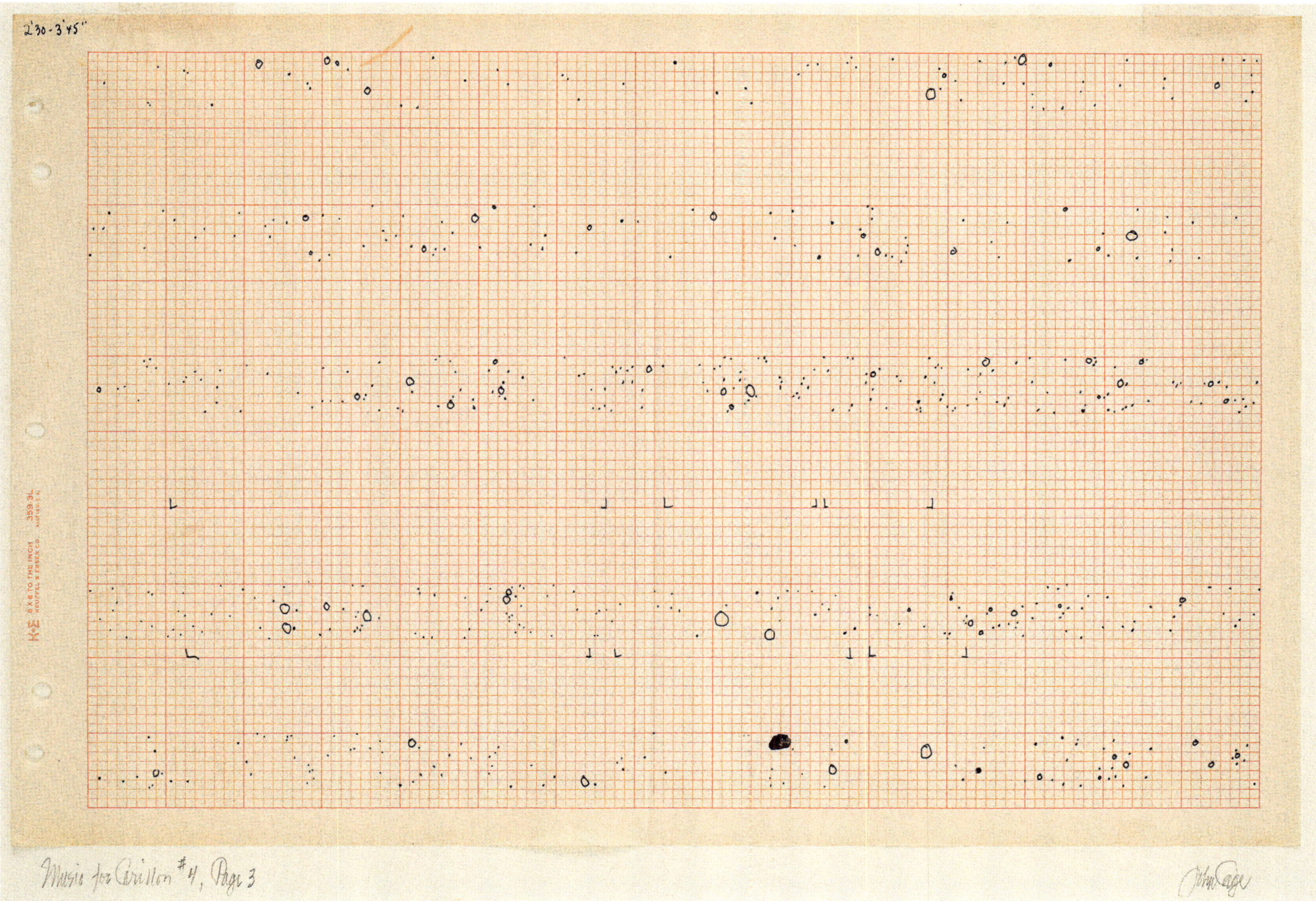

5 John Cage, *Music for Carillon, # 4, Page 3*, 1961

element that was transformed into a source of meaning and hence into an art of building only in the aesthetic order.

> Let us recognize that the mechanistic principle of order overemphasizes the materialistic and functionalist factors. It fails to satisfy our feeling that means must be subsidiary to ends and our desire for dignity and value. The idealistic principle of order, however, with its overemphasis on the ideal and the formal, satisfies neither our interest in truth and simplicity nor our practical sense.
> So we shall emphasize the organic principle of order that makes the parts meaningful and measurable while determining their relationship to the whole.[14]

Grid and order condition each other in the architecture of the Neue Nationalgalerie, but at no point to the extent that the monotony of a mathematically calculated basic grid is felt in the built space. Ludwig Mies van der Rohe was concerned with "higher unity," which he sought in the form of the square, whose properties have an immediately evident and invariable shape. He spoke rather of an order—an order that opens up the radiance of truth in beauty.[15]

1 Ludwig Mies van der Rohe, "Bürohaus," G 1 (July 1923), p. 3, translated as "The Office Building" in Fritz Neumeyer, *The Artless Word: Mies van der Rohe on the Building Art*, trans. Mark Jarzombek (Cambridge, MA: The MIT Press, 1991), p. 241.
2 Peter Carter uses the example of the Convention Hall to show how Mies developed a building independently of constructive structure, proportion, and form; see Peter Carter, *Mies van der Rohe at Work* (London: Phaidon, 1999), p. 102.
3 Carter, *Mies van der Rohe at Work*, p. 96.
4 In the presentation portfolio of the design for the Neue Nationalgalerie from 1963, a grid measuring 90 by 90 centimeters is indicated; except for the floor slabs of 120 by 120 centimeters, all of the dimensions of the Neue Nationalgalerie, apart from the ceiling modules on the lower floor, can be divided by both 90 and 120.
5 Carter, *Mies van der Rohe at Work*, p. 9.
6 The use of the basic grid of 120 centimeters does not result in a square form everywhere. For example, the distances between the supports on the lower floor are regular at 720 centimeters, but the wall partitions do not form square spaces.
7 See the text by Dirk Lohan in the present volume, pp. 58–63.
8 In a telephone call with the present author on June 12, 2020, Dirk Lohan reported that Mies had wanted to use Crown Hall's distribution of windows according to the golden ratio for the Neue Nationalgalerie as well. When requested to reduce the construction costs of that building on the IIT campus in Chicago, he responded by shortening the façade by one foot—an arbitrary modification that resulted in a change in the calculation but not in the optics. This example demonstrates that the grid was merely a means to an end in order to produce an order that was beholden only to aesthetic sense.
9 Ludwig Mies van der Rohe, "Notes for Lectures," in Neumeyer, *The Artless Word*, pp. 268–79, esp. p. 272.
10 Ludwig Mies van der Rohe, "Inaugural Address as Director of Architecture at Armour Institute of Technology" (1938), in Neumeyer, *The Artless Word*, pp. 316–17, esp. p. 316.
11 The eponymous exhibition in 1966 presented the contemporaneous sculpture of Minimal Art in a museum for the first time. *Primary Structures* was curated by Kynaston McShine at the Jewish Museum in New York.
12 Christopher Dell, "Indeterminacy and Grid," in *Das Arbeitende Konzert / The Working Concert* (Leipzig: Spector Books, 2020), p. 160.
13 John Cage, quoted in Branden W. Joseph, "John Cage and the Architecture of Silence," *October* 81 (Summer 1997), pp. 81–104, esp. p. 85.
14 Mies van der Rohe, "Inaugural Address," in Neumeyer, *The Artless Word*, p. 317.
15 Ibid.

TOILETTEN
REST ROOMS
Tickets

The Interior Design

Martin Reichert

All his life, Ludwig Mies van der Rohe understood and planned his buildings as a whole. In addition to the furniture, he paid particular attention to his interiors, which went far beyond the usual fittings. From his early villas by way of his prototypical buildings of the 1920s to the icons of his American output, the interior played a key role. In the Barcelona Pavilion of the International Exposition of 1929, nothing was exhibited: the exhibit was the architecture and its interior.

The particular value that Mies attributed to materials and their joining came naturally to him. As he was from a family of stone masons, he had acquired knowledge of natural stone and how to work it. He never studied architecture but was completely self-taught, after being trained in the crafts and applied arts. Mies was convinced that "[t]he building art begins with the *careful* fitting of two bricks."[1]

It is not just the quality of the materials used in his buildings that is impressive, but also the high level of precision with which they have been worked. "Both new materials and new construction techniques are not necessarily signs of superior quality. What matters is the right application. Each material is only valued by what we make of it."[2] His famous maxim "God is in the details," refers precisely to the art of execution and joinery.

His years of apprenticeship in Berlin started with Bruno Paul, one of the important reformist architects and a representative of Neue Sachlichkeit (New Objectivity) before the First World War. Simultaneously, he was in demand as a furniture and interior designer for luxurious villas, country homes, and transatlantic liners for the Lloyd shipping company. Eventually, Mies switched to the studio of Peter Behrens and he came to understand the prototypical modern architect and industrial designer. Both positions were characterized by universalist architects who practiced design within the full spectrum of its applications and came—as Mies did—from the applied arts and spatial art. This influence was continued and reinforced at the Bauhaus. The science of materials and its application in modern design and architecture influenced all of the stages of education there, from the preliminary course to the master classes. The many years of collaboration with Lilly Reich intensified his understanding of objects and, above all, of textiles. One should consider the Barcelona Pavilion and also their important joint projects for exhibition and trade fairs. In an early interior design, curtains were already employed as elements shaping space. In 1927, Mies codesigned with Reich a stand for the Berlin trade fair *Die Mode der Dame* (Fashion for Women).

The stand, used for the *Café Samt und Seide* (Velvet and Silk Café), was spatially articulated solely by lengths of fabric. Silk and velvet fabrics hung down from straight and curved tubular steel at different heights forming various zones. In residential buildings, such as the Villa Tugendhat in Brno (1928–30), Mies also employed curtains as partitions and sunshades.

Mies's aesthetic is characterized by a kind of "elemental minimalism." His entire oeuvre is marked by reduction of means and decisive use of precious materials such as the legendary onyx wall of the Barcelona Pavilion or the radial partitions of Makassar ebony in the Villa Tugendhat. Rather than diversity, Mies very consciously relied on the "elemental" effect of a few materials to characterize the space. In the Farnsworth House, the floor covering is bright travertine, which together with the steel façade painted white gives the building a dignified radiance. In the legendary Four Seasons restaurant in the Seagram Building, it was the full-height wooden walls that lent elegance to the dining rooms. In the hall of the Neue Nationalgalerie, Mies contrasted the gray stone floor and the almost black steel roof with a complementary color harmony of green marble and reddish-brown oak.

The elemental aspect of Mies's thoughts is also expressed in repetition. The solutions developed in the early buildings of his American oeuvre increasingly assumed a normative quality. Building typologies, constructions parts, elements, and details gradually came together into a master's canon, which was repeated, varied, rearranged, and refined in numerous projects of the 1960s, on a large scale. Many elements and details of the interior design had been employed in other projects before or in parallel with the Neue Nationalgalerie. Crown Hall of the IIT in Chicago (1952–56) in particular and the interiors of the pavilions of the Federal Center in Chicago (planning: 1959–62) and of the Toronto-Dominion Centre (planning: 1963–64) were all designed around the same time as the Nationalgalerie. They remain very close to it, both in terms of material palette and in the intrinsic details of the design solutions.

Nevertheless, in Mies's work everything is always laid out and all aspects planned in great detail specifically for this particular building. Of the forty-three construction documents from Mies van der Rohe's studio, more than three-quarters relate to themes of fit out and interior (A 9–A 43). The planning addresses all of the themes and trades, encompassing installation plans, details of furniture, drawings of escape routes, and the building signage. In terms of space, too, the planning encompasses the entire project—from the outdoor areas, with a precise selection of trees and plants, down to the last corners of the nonpublic working areas. By carefully checking the workshop planning of the firms responsible, inspecting samples of materials and workmanship, and by approving products—all accompanied by the regular presence of the project leader, Mies's grandson Dirk Lohan, on the building site—the architects managed to supervise the exact realization of their planning thoroughly and to have a direct influence on the quality of its implementation (figs. 1, 2).

If comparing a photograph of the hall after the completion of the shell and the steel façade (fig. 3), one is astonished first by the almost imperceptible changes (ill. pp. 68–69). The interior design is like a delicate veil draped over the floor and the two pillars. Only the curtain and the two cloakrooms are added as additional spatial elements. Even after the interior design was complete, the hall continued to be dominated by the unclad, primary architecture (fig. 4). In contrast to the pavilions of the Toronto-Dominion Centre and the Federal Center, its use as a museum required fewer built-ins than the counter hall of a post office or bank. This enabled Mies to leave the universal space in its great purity and emptiness.

The natural-stone slabs of the terrace continue into the interior of the hall. They are not so much a floor covering as part of the podium from whose plateau the hall rises up. Initially, dark-gray natural stone (Swedish granite or southern German sandstone) was to be used as cladding for the podium. In June 1964, Mies selected a cream-white Roman travertine, but it proved difficult to acquire in sufficient

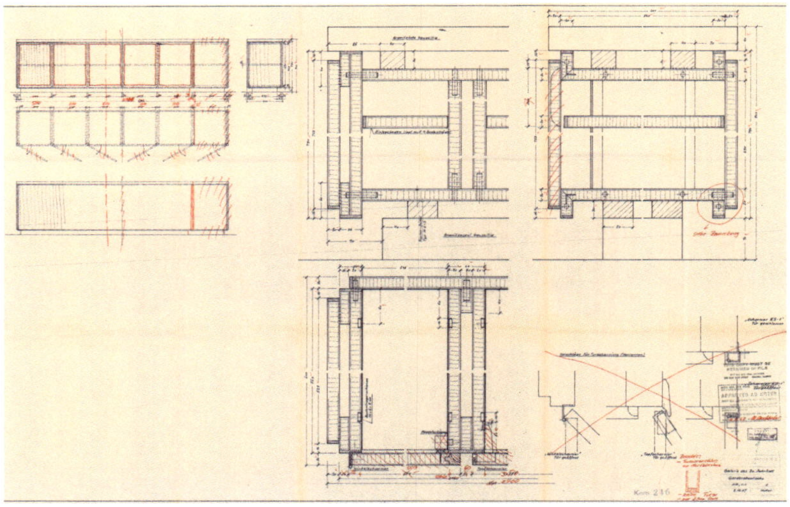

1 Working plan of the cloakroom with the inspection notes of Mies van der Rohe's office, 1967

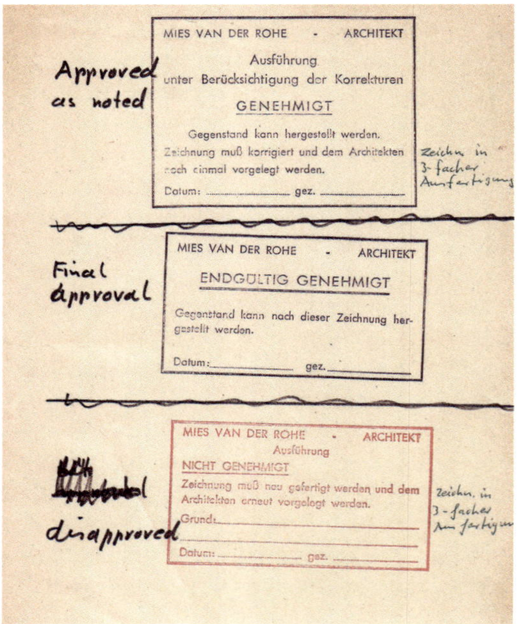

2 Mies van der Rohe's inspection stamp for approving the work of subcontractors, 1966

3 Exhibition hall of the Neue Nationalgalerie under construction, 1967

4 Ludwig Mies van der Rohe, Neue Nationalgalerie, photo montage with marbled paper and wood veneer, 1967–68

quantities. In the autumn of the same year, the Senate proposed an alternative pattern of bright-gray granite from northern Bavaria (Epprechtstein), which was approved. In fact, the majority of the granite was ultimately obtained from Strzegom (formerly Striegau) in Lower Silesia as part of a German-Polish trade agreement. The slabs for the terrace were roughened to make them nonslip, whereas those in the hall were ground, but not polished, so that they could be cleaned more easily. Despite the differences in surfaces, the goal was to achieve a look that was quasi homogenous so that the interior and exterior would perfectly match.

In contrast to the Federal Center in Chicago, the steel beams of the coffered ceiling of the Nationalgalerie are not hidden by a suspended ceiling but are left visible and coated dark gray (fig. 5). This solution would eventually be adopted shortly thereafter in the pavilion of the Toronto-Dominion Centre (fig. 6).

In January 1964, Gene Summers from Mies's office wrote a letter to the structural engineers in which he conveyed his intention to leave the construction of the steel exposed inside and outside for the first time.[3] In October of that same year, he decided that a black gridded roof should be hung in the coffers of the steel construction, both to block the sight of the technical installations above it and to serve as a holder for four downlights per field.[4] The grid of aluminum slats was placed 30 centimeters above the lower flange, which emphasized the continuity of the structure of the steel roof when seen from below. The (nearly) 800 downlights are so narrowly focused that the overall impression of the blackness of the roof is not impaired by the lighting. Despite the many installations, the hall ceiling looks coherent due to the dominating gridiron.

The two full-height wall pillars placed freely in the hall to house the installation shafts are clad with delicate, dark-green Greek marble from Tinos. Mies had used this stone before, prominently in the Barcelona Pavilion (fig. 7) and repeatedly for pillars and wall slabs in realized buildings from the 1940s onward (Seagram Building, 900–910 Lake Shore Drive, 2400 Lakeview Apartments, pavilion of the Toronto-Dominion Centre (fig. 6). The project leader, Dirk Lohan, recalls this marble, which has been quarried since antiquity

5 Ludwig Mies van der Rohe, Federal Center, Chicago, Illinois, interior of the pavilion

6 Ludwig Mies van der Rohe, Toronto-Dominion Centre, interior of the pavilion

7 Ludwig Mies van der Rohe, Barcelona Pavilion, International Exposition of 1929

8 Ludwig Mies van der Rohe, Interior of Crown Hall, campus of the Illinois Institute of Technology, Chicago, Illinois

on the island of Tinos and features a refined pattern of white veins, lending it a vivacious character:

> My grandfather wanted to bring the colour green into the hall, without it competing with the paintings exhibited. We were familiar with Tinos marble, of course. In Italy, I picked out blocks with the intention of having as little grain as possible in the cut slabs. I came to an agreement with the Berlin company installing the marble that the slabs would not be installed with the grain in mirror symmetry but in a simple sequence. As a result, there are no symmetrical, decorative forms, just a slow shifting of the grain from slab to slab.[5]

The cloakrooms, arranged symmetrically in relation to the east–west axis, are not interpreted as part of the primary architecture of the hall as a result of their low height (2.8 meters) and the selected material. Three long partition walls enclose the cloakrooms and also conceal the freight elevator in the southern cloakroom and the cleaning-supply room in the northern cloakroom. The articulation by means of partitions employs large-format panels with precious veneers that vary slightly in appearance. Mies repeats the wooden partition halls on the ground floor of Crown Hall almost literally (fig. 8).

Teak had originally been planned for the wooden parts, and it was not until November 1967 that it was decided to use the English brown oak that Mies had selected for nearly all of his American buildings, even if it was difficult to obtain in Germany. It is a type of oak that has been permanently stained by the beefsteak fungus. Its broad medullary rays look like bright, shining bands when cut radially. Just how important the specific appearance of the wood elements were to Mies and his office is evident from the fact that Lohan traveled to England to personally select the veneer patterns from the William Mallinson & Sons timber company.

At the opening of the building in 1968, a light, semitransparent curtain was hung on three sides of the hall. Previously, in 1963, the Senate expressed the need for a curtain to provide protection against glare and sunlight, to reduce ultraviolet radiation, and to help with climate control. Disagreement over the position of the curtain in relation to the ventilation outlets along the façade led to criticism of the planning. After a study trip to Houston with members of the Stiftung Preussischer Kulturbesitz (Prussian Cultural Heritage Foundation, SPK), the director general at the time, Stephan Waetzoldt, asked Mies van der Rohe in a personal letter (December 1965) to take up the planning again.[6] In his reply of February 1966, Mies addressed Waetzoldt's query: "As you can see, I have not abandoned the idea of the curtain. A carefully selected curtain would not only solve the sunshade problem but also improve the architectural appearance of the large hall in an agreeable fashion. Whatever we plan for solar protection in this location may not under any circumstances detract from the structural clarity and must always read as an independent addition to the building."[7]

As a soft flowing element, the curtains in the exhibition hall and in the basement form a counterpart to the strict geometry and the hard, static materials such as steel, glass, and natural stone. The fabric selected was "Sapphire" from Knoll International. This light-gray polyester weave resembles a light batiste (plane weave) in its texture, transparency, and matte finish.

Even with the curtains closed, the transparency of this fabric preserved the visual relationship between the interior and the urban space, of vital importance to Mies. Historical photographs reveal the strong presence of the curtains and their immense influence on the effect of the hall by day and by night (figs. 9, 10).

The original curtains were characterized by an off-the-rack draping that ensured a regular, wavelike fall of the fabric. The lengths of fabric totaled nearly 3,000 square meters and were moved by electric motors. The parked and stacked positions of the individual curtains were situated near the cloakrooms and in front of the western façade to the left and right. The eastern façade facing Potsdamer Strasse did not have a curtain, so as to avoid the revolving doors. The semitransparent curtain was replaced in the late 1970s by a more solid fabric that allowed less light into the hall. That made special exhibitions with higher conservational requirements possible, but because this solution was completely counter to the idea of the building, the curtains were ultimately removed completely at the end of the 1990s. For the reopening in the summer of 2021, new curtains were produced by Knoll based on an original reference sample. The return of the curtains is an important element of restoring the original look of the large hall.

As an element of continuity, the granite floor covering continues across the two stairways into the lower foyer and from there into the temporary exhibition space and up to the threshold of the exhibition rooms. The steel stairways placed freely in the room repeat, almost like a quotation, the stairs of Crown Hall (fig. 11).

The floor for the collection is completely different in character from the light-flooded hall. The walls and ceilings are immaterial and left in abstract white out of consideration for the art. Unlike the hall, the building shell is almost entirely clad. Only the plaster-covered reinforced-concrete supports give, here and there, a suggestion of the tectonics of the building (figs. 12, 13). Apart from the enfilade along the sculpture garden, the rooms receive no natural light, giving them an introverted character. Visible materials are only found with the wood components made of brown oak, which provide striking accents in nearly all the spaces: as ticket counters in the foyer, built-in furniture in the temporary exhibition space, frames of the glass elements of the doors, door leaves in the public areas, floorboards of the exhibition space, and furnishings in the administration offices.

The early designs planned for a bright terrazzo floor in the spaces for the collection, which was to be divided into 1.2-meter squares by aluminum moldings and thus follow the grid of the granite slabs in the sculpture garden and the lower foyer. The ceilings of the exhibition were, by contrast, conceived as jointless, abstract flat ceilings (fig. 14). In the course of subsequent planning, the design was, in a sense, reversed. The technical requirements for the ceiling—especially the integration of lighting for the rooms and the exhibitions, as well as an air-inlet grille—but also the desire for flexible use made a modular ceiling system necessary. After experiments with perforated-panel systems in metal, wood, and plaster, the decision was made in 1966 to use uniform ceiling panels of composite wood, painted white and measuring 60 by 60 centimeters. To achieve a calmer spatial effect and improve the acoustics, a decision had been made

9 Exhibition hall of the Neue Nationalgalerie with curtains, 1968

10 *Wilhelm Lehmbruck* exhibition, 1973

at a planning meeting in Chicago in November 1965, at which the Berlin clients were present, to install wall-to-wall carpeting.[8] The bouclé carpet of pure virgin wool continues the structure and color of the immediately adjacent granite coverings with its "salt-and-pepper" pattern in gray and white, while ensuring muted acoustics and being very comfortable to walk on with its 10-millimeter-tall pile on a 5-millimeter felt underlay. In creating a uniform view from the garden, this carpet was also used in the two rooms for the administration. The carpets were replaced several times over the years as a result of heavy wear from museum operations, most recently after the MoMA exhibition (2004). As part of the renovation, the manufacturer commissioned in 1967, Ankerwerke, produced a new carpet in visual reference to the original from the construction period but using a sturdy wool-and-synthetic blend.

The presentation portfolio of 1963 shows full-height partition walls in precious wood in a symmetrical arrangement in the large exhibition space next to the sculpture garden. The freestanding exhibition walls were later realized as a carpenter's wooden-stand structure and planked with plywood painted white. Their dimensions and arrangement are based on the grid of the modular ceiling. Shadow gaps at both floor and ceiling level identify the partitions as nonbearing walls. Lighting them with wallwashers that run along the wall further heightens the effect of the panes. At the Hilton Hotel in April 1967, in the presence of Mies and the SPK, a model study was presented of the arrangement of the partition walls in the basement as the basis for planning and discussion. The idea was to divide the large exhibition space into three areas, which would correspond to different exhibition conditions in terms of lighting and spatial qualities: the "large pillar hall" in the central area and the "cabinet wing" in the southern and northern areas.[9]

The subdividing of the 2,200-square-meter-large exhibition space with its open plan and rhythms created by freestanding I- and T-shaped partition walls has essentially proven its worth in recent decades. Over the course of the thorough renovation, the original layout was restored. Mies had wanted the plywood of the partition walls to be covered with linen. A lighting test conducted with paintings on site in

11 Stairs of Crown Hall, campus of the Illinois Institute of Technology, Chicago, Illinois

12 Large exhibition room on the lower floor of the Neue Nationalgalerie with the presentation of the collection, 1968

13 Large exhibition room on the lower floor of the Neue Nationalgalerie, 1967

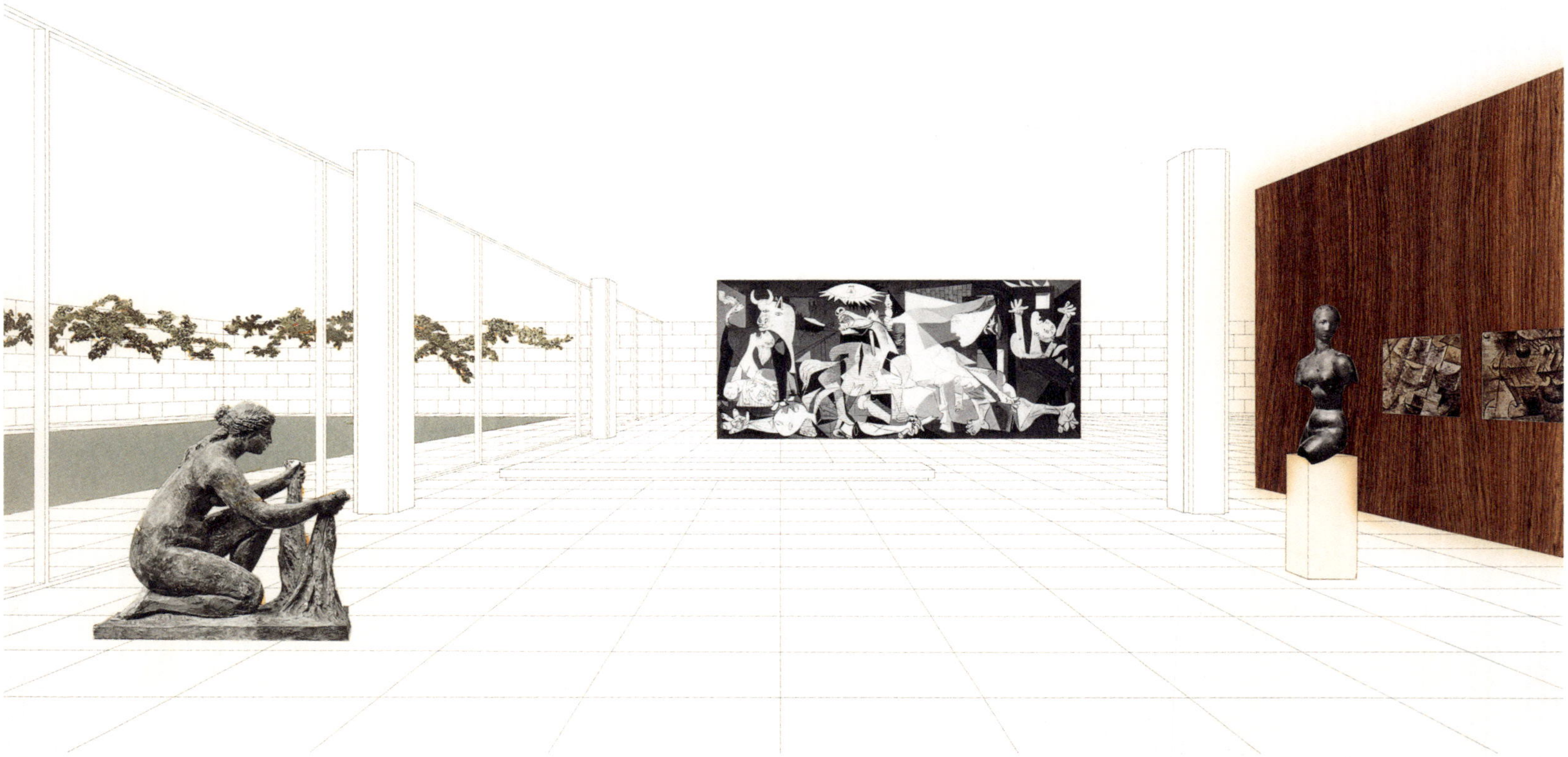

14 Design for the collection rooms of the Neue Nationalgalerie by Ludwig Mies van der Rohe, 1963

the autumn of 1966 made it clear that undesirable shadows were created by the picture frames, so it was decided to use a coarse woodchip wallpaper from the firm Erfurt, which was then also used in the temporary exhibition space and the administrative offices.[10]

The exhibition lighting is innovative, with downlights and wallwashers developed especially for the Neue Nationalgalerie. Mies applied his own experiences with the light planner Richard Kelly and adapted them in collaboration with the German light planner Hans Theo von Malotki of Interlumen Lichtarchitektur GmbH. The special lamps from the American manufacturer Edison Price Lighting produced by the German manufacturer Semperlux AG under a licensing agreement were based on prototypes built in 1965.

The attitude of the architects was pragmatic with regard to many of the planning themes on the floor for the permanent collection. When it was considered acceptable from a design perspective, they dispensed with custom manufacturing for specific objects and accepted standard, commercially available products. For the public restrooms, the architects largely followed the Senate's proposals and chose inexpensive models for the ceramic sanitary equipment and the fittings. Regardless, the consideration of detail in the sanitary facilities testifies to high design expectations. In the planning, particular emphasis was placed on the consistent use of complete (uncut) tiles and continuous joints between the wall and floor. The medium-sized mosaic tiles, 5 by 5 centimeters each, were delivered by Villeroy & Boch. For the floor, gray unglazed fine stoneware was used; for the walls, white, glazed tiles with delicate nuances of color.

Compared to contemporaneous museum buildings in West Germany, the Neue Nationalgalerie is a high-tech building. Mies pursued the state of the art in the United States and tried to realize that despite the restrictive conditions in the zoned city of West Berlin. The building has a very large amount of installation equipment. The modern climate-control, lighting, and security technology nevertheless remain invisible to avoid detracting from the purism of the architecture and competing with the exhibited works of art. All of the walls and floors are almost completely free of visible technical components. The building technology is concentrated in the ceiling, but thanks to the grid design it has very little visual presence.

Whereas Mies subordinated the aesthetic of the basement entirely to the presentation of the collection, he designed the exhibition hall as a stage. The cloakrooms in brown oak and the marble-clad shafts are like a backdrop that articulates the expansive space, which gets lost in the cityscape of Berlin in the distance. Mies contrasted the modern promise of steel-and-glass architecture with traditional trades (carpentry and stonemasonry). The result was a symbiosis of his native European roots and the progress he made in America, his adoptive country.

This article is based on an examination and evaluation of the planning documents and text sources conducted in 2012–14 by my colleague Marianne Akay in the archives of the Museum of Modern Art, New York; the Library of Congress, Washington, DC; and various Berlin archives.

1 Ludwig Mies van der Rohe, quoted in Christian Norberg-Schultz, "A Talk with Mies van der Rohe," in Fritz Neumeyer, *The Artless Word: Mies van der Rohe on the Building Art*, trans. Mark Jarzombek (Cambridge, MA: The MIT Press, 1991), pp. 338–39, esp. p. 338 (emphasis in the original).
2 Ibid., p. 336.
3 Gene Summers to the structural engineer Dienst & Richter, January 20, 1964, Ludwig Mies van der Rohe Archive, Museum of Modern Art, New York (hereafter MvdR Archive), correspondence folder (CF) 10-0009.
4 Meeting minutes by the Senatsverwaltung für Bauen und Wohnen, October 5, 1964, MvdR Archive, CF 20-0024.
5 Dirk Lohan in conversation with Constanze von Marlin, February 26, 2016.
6 Stephan Waetzoldt to Ludwig Mies van der Rohe, December 7, 1965, MvdR Archive, CF 14-0006.
7 Ludwig Mies van der Rohe to Stephan Waetzoldt, February 28, 1966, MvdR Archive, CF 14-0017.
8 Meeting minutes, November 15, 1965, MvdR Archive, CF 14-0004.7.
9 Mr. Haftmann SPK to Dirk Lohan, May 19, 1967, MvdR Archive, CF 26-0008.1.
10 Mr. Grote SPK to Dirk Lohan, May 18, 1967, MvdR Archive, CF 26-0005.2.

The Furniture

Furniture in the Room, Furniture for Rooms

Christiane Lange

Immediately at the entrance of the Neue Nationalgalerie, one can, with a little luck, see it: the Barcelona chair, Ludwig Mies van der Rohe's most famous item of furniture, an icon of modernism, exhibited at documenta III and, ever since, a statement in any interior. On a dark carpet of around 5 by 7 meters, several chairs are arranged with stools along with two Tugendhat tables to form a spacious group. It is an area for resting, waiting, or conversing. That is what Mies van der Rohe planned it for—and may it always be so now and again in the future (fig. 1).

When the Neue Nationalgalerie opened in 1968, the Barcelona chair was already a classic or, to express it more modestly, a piece of furniture that was nearly forty years old. Mies had designed it in 1929 for the pavilion of the German Reich at the Barcelona International Exposition, not as a throne for the king and queen of Spain, as speculated in earlier scholarship, but indeed as a "monumental object," as Mies expressed it in 1964. He said that he needed seating furniture for the pavilion that unfurled a space-shaping force without blocking "the special [meaning arguably "spatial"] flow of the building."

Giving furniture a quality that determined the space was a logical consequence of Mies's concept of the open, flowing space, which he had developed since the mid-1920s above all in the context of exhibition architectures such as the *Glasraum* (Glass Room) in Stuttgart and the *Café Samt und Seide* (Velvet and Silk Café) in Berlin. His concept in a nutshell was to cease articulating certain areas with walls and doors, instead using ensembles of furniture to mark the various functions without breaking up the spatial continuum. The furniture became part of the architecture; consequently, furnishings became a regular feature of the planning commissions that Mies and his firm carried out. More than any other item of his furniture, the Barcelona chair in future would fulfill this function not only in private residences but also and above all in the stately lobbies of his apartment blocks, the university buildings of the Illinois Institute of Technology (fig. 5), and in the exhibition hall of the Nationalgalerie.

In Mies's new spatial concept, however, it was not just furniture that held a designated function but also walls. In the mid-1920s, the architect experimented for the first time with mobile wall elements. In 1927, he provided the residents of his housing block in the Weissenhof housing development in Stuttgart with wooden wall elements with which they could subdivide the floor space according to their needs (fig. 2). In the residence of Hermann Lange in Krefeld one year later, he integrated a detachable wooden wall between the dining room and hall. On special occasions, it was a simple matter to remove it and thus cause the two rooms to merge into one. He treated these wall elements like furniture that could be moved as necessary. When steel-skeleton construction made it possible to separate the wall and the load-bearing structure entirely, Mies began to place wall elements of precious woods or stone in the room. Furniture and partition walls now marked spatial zones.

This is the tradition to which the two large wooden cubes with expansive wall elements in the exhibition hall of the Neue Nationalgalerie also belong (fig. 3). These forms, just under 3 meters tall, house cloakrooms. Without any structural connection to the ceiling and floor, they look like furniture placed in the room. A collage from the time of the construction of the Nationalgalerie clarifies its central task of spatial composition (fig. 4, p. 195). And it illustrates a second central aspect of Mies's architecture: it shows the great importance he attributed to the material itself. In a kind of counterpoint, he contrasted the strict architectural order of the hall with the delicate structure of brown wood veneer as "natural" material. (The grain of the marble cladding the service ducts in the rear of the hall performs a similar function, by the way.)

The transparent exhibition hall, which Mies placed on a podium as a pure architectonic structure—like an ancient temple—could not be more different from the introverted basement with its courtyard-like sculpture garden. If the exhibition hall was to offer "rich and new possibilities for structuring exhibitions," as Mies van der Rohe wrote, then the basement, which is shielded from the outside, emphasized contemplative viewing of the permanent collection.

Anyone arriving in the basement via one of the two stairways—a self-citation of the architect modeled on the Arts Club of Chicago (1951)—will experience a transition from

1 Exhibition hall of the Neue Nationalgalerie with seating group and cloakrooms, 1968

room to rooms. In the interior design, a change occurs from pointed placements to furnishings according to use. In the perception of visitors, the basement is dominated by flat steel. In the stairwell, the furniture ensemble of the entrance to the exhibition hall is repeated. Several Tugendhat chairs, also executed in flat steel, have been added over the course of time. In the presentation of the collection, Barcelona stools were used as well as benches derived from them that were designed around the time of the building's construction and produced in a small series of nineteen, presumably exclusively for the Neue Nationalgalerie. Beginning with the Barcelona stools, the seating area was extended by about four times and was now based on four pairs of skids. Their all-around use and placement in the middle of the exhibition area is oriented toward forms of traditional museum furnishings (fig. 4).

All of the chairs, stools, and benches of flat steel were supplied by the American company Knoll International, which produced them by series, in some cases since the 1950s. The names of the models commonly used today can be traced back to Knoll, not Mies, and are aimed more at placing the furniture in question in the context of an interesting project than at historical accuracy. Apart from the benches, they date from the late 1920s when Mies designed them and had them made in the context of just a few architectural projects. The technical working out of the designs was done in close collaboration with the professionals who were manufacturing them. Prototypes were built and discussed in the office. This process was carried out in parallel with the production of the first furniture, which is why the early examples that are now so sought after by collectors have differences in construction and look. The most recent research on Mies van der Rohe's furniture designs concludes that just over twenty-five Barcelona chairs had been manufactured prior to the Second World War; the number of stools and tables is probably even smaller.

Mies's recourse to furniture concepts from the 1920s, his Berlin period, had nothing to do with sentimentality. Rather, the entire furniture oeuvre of Mies van der Rohe dates exclusively from this period. Along with a few later enhancements, this repertoire was reused regularly by him and his team until

2 Ludwig Mies van der Rohe, mobile wall element, Weissenhof housing development, Stuttgart, after 1927

3 Cloakroom of brown oak designed by Ludwig Mies van der Rohe, 2014

4 Ludwig Mies van der Rohe, benches in the large exhibition room on the lower floor, Neue Nationalgalerie, 1969

5 Ludwig Mies van der Rohe, seating group in the School of Social Service Administration, University of Chicago, 1968

6 Access to the director's offices of the Neue Nationalgalerie, 2021

the end of his long career. At the same time, the diverse innovations in terms of material and form that his colleagues produced did not influence him, nor did the pioneering questioning of modernism from the 1960s onward.

Only after Mies moved to the United States did he begin collaborating with Florence and Walter Knoll to produce series of designs of flat-steel furniture. Florence Knoll had studied under Mies at the Illinois Institute of Technology in Chicago and from the 1940s developed a furniture program with leading designers of the time for the company founded by her husband. As of the 1950s, Mies's flat-steel designs gradually went into production; tubular-steel pieces and several upholstered furniture items followed.

The fame of his flat-steel furniture and its presence in the public areas of the museum distract from the fact that most of the furniture and built-ins of the Neue Nationalgalerie were made of wood: writing desks, library furniture, cabinets, and display tables, as well as doors and door frames, are executed in wood, as are the sales counters for postcards and catalogues.

As one would expect, the rooms for the administration received the greatest attention when it came to furnishings. Even the path to it was extraordinary, as Mies had placed its stately main entrance in the collection area of the basement (fig. 6). The concept of his design was that guests of the direction would meander through the presentation and arrive at the so-called lobby of the administration at its left flank. In front of a full-height wooden wall, a reception area with a small desk was planned here: a workplace with little natural light from an era of minimal occupational safety regulations. This wooden wall—with similar paneling and the brown-oak veneer of the wooden cubes in the exhibition hall—provides a privacy screen for the entrances to the offices behind it. A cabinet was later added behind it. According to the surviving plans for the furnishings, to the left and right of this entrance would stand two small seating groups with Barcelona chairs and a Tugendhat table where waiting guests would sit. The main entrance of the administration was, however, rarely used in this way. Instead, the side entrance at the western access ramp mutated into the entrance to the administration areas.

Like the flat-steel pieces, the wooden furniture and built-ins of the Nationalgalerie are based on types of furniture that had been developed forty years earlier. The exhibition and furniture designer Lilly Reich (1885–1947) played a central role in the creation of this repertoire. From 1926 to 1939, she had a personal and professional relationship with Mies. Especially in the area of exhibition and furniture design, the two worked closely together. Reports by former colleagues and students testify to Mies's respect for Reich's judgment and the intense exchange between the two on all questions of design. Although they took separate paths in the field of tubular-steel furniture—in which Lilly Reich was, by the way, the only woman—the authorship of the furniture in wood or a combination of wood and tubular steel is often not clearly identifiable. Scholars have therefore come to speak of joint authorship here.

The first designs for wooden furniture that should be attributed to Mies were produced around 1925–26 for his own apartment in Berlin. They include a wooden table that became the blueprint for nearly all of his future wooden tables that he and also Lilly Reich designed for their interiors. The principle of the design is based on a tabletop with a frame supported by four legs placed in the corners. The tabletop, frame, and legs have flush joints. Not only the construction of the table is striking but also the use of veneer. It runs vertically on the legs, frame, and edge of the tabletop and completely conceals the joints beneath it. These tables look as if they had been carved from a block of wood. Mies and Reich designed numerous variations on this construction, including writing desks with and without drawers, heavy expandable tables, slender dining tables, and square bridge and tea tables.

Mies and his coworkers also applied this design principle to the desks in the library of the Neue Nationalgalerie. Six reading desks in brown-oak were built. The tabletops are covered with imitation leather (fig. 7). Three desks with additional drawers and a rear wall were used in the offices and the reception area.

The tables for the director's office and the adjoining conference room can be traced back to a refined type that Mies and Reich first conceived in 1929 under the influence

7 Ludwig Mies van der Rohe, reading desk, 2021

of the design possibilities of tubular steel. A worktable with two drawers was produced for the living room of the Tugendhat House (fig. 8). The carcass is blocky in design, the drawers are flush, and the veneer is applied vertically, as is the case with all of Mies's wooden furniture. In contrast to the older design, the carcass is now supported by four receded tubular-steel legs. Reflections on its shiny surfaces make it appear to dissolve optically. The desk seems light, as if it were floating. Lilly Reich developed a whole series of furniture during this period in which she combined tubular-steel elements with the wooden elements they supported. She listed as her designs shelves, vitrines, and the day bed based on this same principle now manufactured by Knoll under Mies's name. But Mies also used this type of table repeatedly: for example, a simple variation with a wooden tabletop in his office and his apartment in Chicago. The forward-looking potential of the simplicity of disassembling and reassembling it was demonstrated for the first time when the furnishings for an apartment for Philip Johnson, which Mies and Reich had designed together in 1930 and produced in Berlin, were shipped to New York.

The director's desk (fig. 9) is largely identical in its construction to the Tugendhat table, which was forty years older. Its carcass is made of brown oak, and only one small detail was added: a pull-out board at the long end on which to rest a stenography pad—a document of the predigital work processes of the 1960s. A second table of the same type but without drawers in the director's office served, for example, as a display table to view portfolios of prints or the like; a third one of twice the size was used in the adjacent conference room. Soon after the Nationalgalerie opened, the second deviation from Mies van der Rohe's planning occurred. Because there were no meetings of this size, the conference room initially provided the director with additional workspace for his extensive publishing activities. Because the lighting was favorable here, the restoration workshop then moved into this space. Then there was no longer any use for the large conference table. It was divided into two square parts, which then found new use as smaller conference tables in the library and in the director's office—now also a conference room. A full-height wall cabinet with a coatrack

8 Ludwig Mies van der Rohe and Lilly Reich, Makassar ebony writing desk for the Tugendhat House, Brünn (now Brno), Czechoslovakia, 1930s

9 Director Werner Haftmann at a tubular-steel writing desk in the Neue Nationalgalerie, 1968

and sink rounded out the furnishings of the office. Its façade with brown-oak veneer and two sets of five doors corresponds to the two other paneled wood walls in the building. The director's room was originally intended to have a seating group with Barcelona chairs and a Tugendhat table for small meetings. The planned version emphasized the director's prestigious position. That did not spare him from working, however: the photograph shows Werner Haftmann at his beautifully designed desk covered with stacks of papers.

The biggest challenge when originally furnishing the Nationalgalerie was the successful opening up of the museum for a broader public. Whereas in the 1960s the focus was still on a relatively small public visiting the permanent collection, today the activities are dominated by changing exhibitions. Large and popular exhibitions and new educational and marketing concepts have considerably increased attendance numbers. The building was and continues to be adapted to higher standards for security, logistics, and inclusion. The ticket desk and the cloakroom have therefore been located in the basement for several years now. In addition, as part of the renovation by David Chipperfield Architects, former storage areas were freed up to provide sufficient space for the museum shop. The square ticket counter—which of course also features brown-oak veneer—has been moved to storage.

All of the other furniture, however, will continue to do in the future what it was designed for: providing employees, guests, and visitors with stools, benches, chairs, tables, and cabinets. The credo of the renovation—"As much Mies as possible"—not only spared the interior design unnecessary modernization but also prevented it from becoming a museum object itself.

Bibliography

Bartsch, Jochen. "Die Ausstattung der Nationalgalerie von Ludwig Mies van der Rohe." Thesis, Fachhochschule Potsdam, FB Architektur und Städtebau, 2005.

Lange, Christiane. "Bestandserfassungen der Möbel der NNG für das Werkverzeichnis der Möbel Mies van der Rohes." Arbeitskreis Werkverzeichnis der Möbel und Möbelzeichnungen von Ludwig Mies van der Rohe, Zentralinstitut für Kunstgeschichte. Munich, 2016 (unpublished).

"The Collaboration between Lilly Reich and Ludwig Mies van der Rohe." In *Mies and Modern Living: Interiors, Furniture, Photography*. Edited by Helmut Reuter and Birgit Schulte. Translated by Paul Aston et al., pp. 194–207. Ostfildern: Hatje Cantz, 2008.

Ludwig Mies van der Rohe & Lilly Reich: Furniture and Interiors. Translated by Allison Plath-Moseley. Exh. cat. Haus Lange, Krefeld. Ostfildern: Hatje Cantz, 2007.

Tegethoff, Wolf. "The Pavilion Chair." In *Mies and Modern Living: Interiors, Furniture, Photography*. Edited by Helmut Reuter and Birgit Schulte, pp. 144–73. Ostfildern: Hatje Cantz, 2008.

The author wishes to thank the following individuals for the information they provided:

Dirk Lohan, grandson of Ludwig Mies van der Rohe and site manager of the NNG project, email to the author, April 26, 2020.

Prof. Jörn Merkert, assistant to Werner Haftmann, 1968–79, email to the author, May 5, 2020.

Roland Sommer, ProDenkmal, email to the author, May 5, 2020.

and sink rounded out the furnishings of the office. Its façade with brown-oak veneer and two sets of five doors corresponds to the two other paneled wood walls in the building. The director's room was originally intended to have a seating group with Barcelona chairs and a Tugendhat table for small meetings. The planned version emphasized the director's prestigious position. That did not spare him from working, however: the photograph shows Werner Haftmann at his beautifully designed desk covered with stacks of papers.

The biggest challenge when originally furnishing the Nationalgalerie was the successful opening up of the museum for a broader public. Whereas in the 1960s the focus was still on a relatively small public visiting the permanent collection, today the activities are dominated by changing exhibitions. Large and popular exhibitions and new educational and marketing concepts have considerably increased attendance numbers. The building was and continues to be adapted to higher standards for security, logistics, and inclusion. The ticket desk and the cloakroom have therefore been located in the basement for several years now. In addition, as part of the renovation by David Chipperfield Architects, former storage areas were freed up to provide sufficient space for the museum shop. The square ticket counter—which of course also features brown-oak veneer—has been moved to storage.

All of the other furniture, however, will continue to do in the future what it was designed for: providing employees, guests, and visitors with stools, benches, chairs, tables, and cabinets. The credo of the renovation—"As much Mies as possible"—not only spared the interior design unnecessary modernization but also prevented it from becoming a museum object itself.

Bibliography

Bartsch, Jochen. "Die Ausstattung der Nationalgalerie von Ludwig Mies van der Rohe." Thesis, Fachhochschule Potsdam, FB Architektur und Städtebau, 2005.

Lange, Christiane. "Bestandserfassungen der Möbel der NNG für das Werkverzeichnis der Möbel Mies van der Rohes." Arbeitskreis Werkverzeichnis der Möbel und Möbelzeichnungen von Ludwig Mies van der Rohe, Zentralinstitut für Kunstgeschichte. Munich, 2016 (unpublished).

"The Collaboration between Lilly Reich and Ludwig Mies van der Rohe." In *Mies and Modern Living: Interiors, Furniture, Photography*. Edited by Helmut Reuter and Birgit Schulte. Translated by Paul Aston et al., pp. 194–207. Ostfildern: Hatje Cantz, 2008.

Ludwig Mies van der Rohe & Lilly Reich: Furniture and Interiors. Translated by Allison Plath-Moseley. Exh. cat. Haus Lange, Krefeld. Ostfildern: Hatje Cantz, 2007.

Tegethoff, Wolf. "The Pavilion Chair." In *Mies and Modern Living: Interiors, Furniture, Photography*. Edited by Helmut Reuter and Birgit Schulte, pp. 144–73. Ostfildern: Hatje Cantz, 2008.

The author wishes to thank the following individuals for the information they provided:

Dirk Lohan, grandson of Ludwig Mies van der Rohe and site manager of the NNG project, email to the author, April 26, 2020.

Prof. Jörn Merkert, assistant to Werner Haftmann, 1968–79, email to the author, May 5, 2020.

Roland Sommer, ProDenkmal, email to the author, May 5, 2020.

The Typeface

Mies van der Rohe's Allzweck Alphabet

Erik Spiekermann

Before computers liberated us from such work, architects learned as part of their studies how to label plans properly. The American architect Francis Ching wrote his lectures in longhand and perfected his writing to the point where he produced an entire book that way, which was printed in facsimile. Under the name Tekton, Ching's hand lettering has been digitized for twenty years, uniting the liveliness of handwriting with the repeatability and technical precision of a computer font (fig. 1).

Because individual expression is not necessarily desirable on building plans, which serve technical communication, architects have preferred to write in capital letters. The tendency to use the basic geometric form, which contradicts the natural flow of writing, and from which our printed texts have long since emancipated themselves, was also the basis for the teaching of lettering at the Bauhaus, which was, of course, also influenced by architects, as its very name makes clear. The Bauhaus produced many interesting typographic experiments, but in the end they only worked as decorative alphabets—there was not a single legible typeface for printing.

Even today, we are often asked to fill out forms in capital letters, because their basic geometric shapes are difficult to subject to a flow of writing that connects the letters. As individual letters, they are easier to distinguish from one another, but more laborious to write. Capital letters need more room than mixed capitalization styles; on building plans and design drawings, however, no extensive texts are written, after all, but rather brief, precise information and above all numbers. Working plans have to be labeled carefully. There are stencils to do this; they make labeling more uniform, though not necessarily easier, since there were (and still are) rules for the sizes and types of lettering as well. The letters of these stencils were always alphabets that were highly reduced geometrically, legible and clear, but at the same time also joyless and suited for no purpose other than standardized labeling.

Architects therefore prefer capitals—uppercase letters still very close to the Roman *capitalis* of two millennia ago. As in architecture, one thing matters above all in typography: when we arrange the black signs, we are articulating the white plane. We are not reading the black—it is invisible, precisely black—but rather the surrounding white. Type designers configure the interiors of letters just as much as their outlines. Architects design interiors for human beings that, from the outside, are called buildings and add to urban space. Because of the monotonous repetition of the same elements, a concrete-slab building seems like a concrete fence with glass surfaces; and one side constructed arhythmically, without contrast and tension, looks like a concrete bunker whose inhabitability one would not like to experience personally. A blank A4 sheet without markings, with much-too-wide lines, a poor construction material (interchangeable fonts such as Arial or Times New Roman), and faulty details (incorrect opening and closing quotation marks, confusion of hyphens and em dashes, improper word divisions, an accent instead of an apostrophe) all call for the wrecking ball, similar to the many buildings constructed according to calculations of width times height times money.

Good typography creates identity for the sender of a text, just as good buildings characterize a city. In both cases, composure is evident from the design and produces confidence or rejection. A well-designed book is more pleasurable to read than an indifferently produced one and is more likely to be worth its price. All trends, as well as the skills of the trades and the culture of the clients, and hence the state of society, leave their mark on typographic products without any delay caused by the process. The state of a society can also be judged by its architecture, but the processes necessary for that take years and decades.

2 Copperplate Gothic, designed by Frederic Goudy for American Type Founders (ATF), 1901, digital version for Linotype

3 Allzweck alphabet, office of Mies van der Rohe, 1960s
The typeface was created by removing the serifs from Copperplate.

4 Allzweck alphabet, 2011, digitized and slightly modified by Ralph du Carrois for the Neue Nationalgalerie

It is obvious that the look of a building that marks our cityscape as strongly as the Neue Nationalgalerie should be designed down to its last detail. Many architects have not let others deprive them of the designing of door handles and window frames, banisters and lighting fixtures. Examples of exterior and interior labeling influenced by the architect are, by contrast, rare.

Ludwig Mies van der Rohe took on that task and had his employee and grandson Dirk Lohan draw up an alphabet that was intended to fulfill all written tasks. In accordance with the tradition described above, the Allzweck (All-Purpose) alphabet consists of capital letters only (fig. 3). And its name is a contradiction in terms, because very few typographic tasks can be fulfilled by capitals alone—though they may suffice for all purposes of labeling buildings.

When designing a typeface there is always one basic conflict: fundamentally, broad forms—especially with capital letters—are more recognizable and hence legible, because larger interiors can be modulated more clearly, and we read the contrast between black and white. Broad letterforms are thus more legible than narrow ones and appear more monumental, and a great museum building is certainly entitled to that. At the same time, however, they need a lot of room. A word such as CLOAKROOM still fits on a door in a legible size, but WEST CONFERENCE ROOM is already more problematic. In a complex airport building, with its many, exacting, and also bilingual signs, a typeface such as the Allzweck alphabet would be out of place. In the spacious and emphatically horizontal Neue Nationalgalerie, by contrast, it underscores the generous, open character of the building (fig. 6).

Dirk Lohan did not allow himself to be influenced at the time by German engineering standards; if he had, then he would have adopted the DIN 1451 typeface, which we Germans recognize from our street and autobahn signage. Instead, he utilized a model that inherently enjoys some prestige. Those who could afford to do so had their calling cards elegantly printed with steel-plate engraving. The letters thus had to be engraved into a steel or copper plate; consequently, the script that still expresses elevated ambition is called copperplate. Its broad letterforms are not suitable for German hyphenated married names, but a classic

5 Ludwig Mies van der Rohe, architect’s plan A 43, Allzweck alphabet, Neue Nationalgalerie, 1965–68

6 Signage in the Neue Nationalgalerie using the Allzweck alphabet, 2021

American name with a middle initial à la John F. Kennedy will still fit on the card—which has to be printed on handmade paper, of course. Dirk Lohan therefore took a copperplate script (fig. 2) and cut off its serifs—that is, those small beginning and ending strokes with which Roman stone carvers already terminated their letters horizontally.

The result is as singular as it is clumsy. When their horizontal terminations are removed, letters with straight sides, such as H or M, seem narrower than before that surgery, whereas the O cannot conceal its recumbent form. Without any stabilizing serifs, nearly all letters totter violently. The head of the S falls to the left; the 2 is also rather buckled. Nearly all horizontal strokes are too bold; the W seems to be one size larger than the V. Many of these awkward-looking forms are surely less obvious when the letters are carved from metal, with a clear depth and a shadow edge, and mounted on walls or other surfaces. There were lead letters as negative on granite, bronze ones as positive on granite, wood, and white walls and as labels on glass. One of just forty-three plans in A0 format was dedicated to the Allzweck alphabet (fig. 5). This illustrates how the architect considered it important that the labeling not be left to some service provider but rather be integrated into the design of the building. Today, this type design by a typographical layman looks a little awkward to experts in the field, but it is also charming.

In a new building from the twenty-first century, this naïveté would be less appropriate. As precise as the steel construction of the building, the revised digital version of the Allzweck alphabet (fig. 4) radiates the same spirit, yet it performs the function of its craft better. We type designers are accustomed to our work being apocryphal: Why should anyone know who has designed the type? If it serves its purpose, then it draws attention to the words, to the text, not to itself. For future visitors to the Neue Nationalgalerie, it will seem as if the lettering has been as thoroughly renovated as the building itself, which today more than ever reflects the intention of the architect who designed this unique building.

The Refurbishment

LEX
PERI UP

When “God Is in the Details”

Restoration projects such as the Neue Nationalgalerie (New National Gallery) depend—rather like archaeological works—on a common agreement about the importance of the building, and a common understanding of its cultural worth and its physical qualities. Despite its relative youth, radical form, and complicated history, it is a testament to the architect Ludwig Mies van der Rohe that the Neue Nationalgalerie is held in such high esteem, not just by historians and architects, but by the people of Berlin. It has been fascinating to see how a modern building from the 1960s is viewed as a monument of cultural significance and should be treated accordingly. Only because of this common respect could our work be regarded with the importance it has been given. Only with this attitude could the decisions be taken so seriously.

Our intention and commitment were to protect, repair, and renew this great building without significant visible alterations while making substantial technical and organizational improvements. Like restoring a 1965 Mercedes, we returned it in perfect condition, appearing as the original but with everything working smoothly. It has been very enjoyable to see that the pieces of a modern building can be granted the same respect as those of a Baroque church or even a Greek temple, with about 35,000 pieces carefully removed, numbered, repaired, and put back in place. This mission was an intricate and delicate task. Perhaps it is a paradox that it will not be evident if we have done our work well.

Of course, it is an exaggeration to say that there are no changes, but the building should not appear any different in its overall effect or idea. It differs in terms of substance and some of its planning. We were making some careful infrastructural interventions, especially in the technical areas and the building’s public amenities. In this distinction lies the fascination of the project and its architectural lesson. Buildings are many things at once: how they appear and how they are made; what they look like and how they feel; their guise and their substance. It is a constant struggle to insist that the physical material qualities really matter, insisting that small decisions, careful work, precision, care, and craft are important to the feeling and experience of a building. In our contemporary society, these qualities are ever more difficult to protect and to argue for.

Mies van der Rohe famously liked to say that “God is in the details.” With that phrase, the architect, who changed the face of modern architecture, reminded us that the big gesture can only be realized, validated, or given meaning through the rigor of its physical realization. The idea is totally dependent on the quality of its physical resolution. The idea finds the most intense manifestation in its making. This is the power of Mies’s great project—a building that has its head in the clouds and its feet firmly on the ground. Its great vision touches us, not just through its lofty ideas, but through its tangible physical qualities—by the order and care for the “stuff” of architecture, and by elevating the practical and prosaic into the realm of ideas.

We have the chance to reaffirm Mies’s ideas through the physical realization of our task, reasserting the importance of making, and perhaps this time we can even put a little more God into some of those details.

David Chipperfield

The Collection

Art of the Twentieth Century

Maike Steinkamp, Dieter Scholz

The collection of twentieth-century art that is now permanently housed at the Neue Nationalgalerie has had a complicated, mutable history. It grew together from two countries, two systems, and two lines of thought. Only after the reunification of the two German states were the holdings of modern art—distributed between East and West Berlin for just over forty years—merged (fig. 1). This reorganization was vehemently debated at the time. Above all, critics saw the integration of the paintings of Bernhard Heisig, Willi Sitte, Werner Tübke, and Wolfgang Mattheuer as exclusively representing the "official" art of the German Democratic Republic (GDR)—and with almost no explanation of the political context in which they had been produced.[1] Moreover, the two art "systems" of the Federal Republic of Germany and the German Democratic Republic were—despite their proximity in the exhibition spaces—clearly separated. A dialogue resulting from designing and interwoven interplay only came about years later in the presentation of the collection under the title *Der geteilte Himmel* (Divided Heaven) in 2011–13.[2]

The first show of the joint collections from East and West in 1993–94 was truly a new beginning. Until that time, the only works on view in the building by Ludwig Mies van der Rohe had been those acquired by West Berlin since 1945, for which the building had been constructed. With the end of the Second World War and the founding of the two German states in 1949, a dual collection structure had formed, resulting from the separation of the (then) Staatliche Museen (National Museums), which were located in both East and West Berlin. From that time forward, collecting was separate in the two parts of the city under different political conditions, guidelines, and strategies.

Two States, Two Collections

In the beginning, it had looked like there was still a joint path. In 1946, the Magistrat (Municipal Administration) of Greater Berlin, which was responsible for the museums, appointed Ludwig Justi director general. He had run the Nationalgalerie from 1909 to 1933 and in 1919 made it the first national museum in the world with a permanent presentation of contemporary art. The focus of this "Neue Abteilung" (Modern Section), which was housed in the former Kronprinzenpalais (Palace of the Crown Prince, a building on the street Unter den Linden), had been German Expressionism (fig. 2). With the takeover of power by the National Socialists in 1933 and their "Entartete Kunst" (Degenerate Art) endeavor in 1937, the collection of modern art was nearly completely dismantled. More than 500 works of art were confiscated from the Nationalgalerie and later sold, traded, or destroyed.[3] Several are still regarded as lost today, surely the most famous example being *Der Turm der blauen Pferde* (The Tower of Blue Horses, 1913) by Franz Marc. Only a few escaped confiscation, thanks to fortunate circumstances, such as Ernst Ludwig Kirchner's *Rheinbrücke in Köln* (Rhine Bridge in Cologne, 1914).

Other works were returned to the Nationalgalerie after the end of the Second World War. For example, Rudolf Belling's abstract sculpture *Dreiklang* (Triad, 1919–24), his *Kopf in Messing* (Head in Brass, 1925), and the painting *Teltow II* (1918) by Lyonel Feininger were, in 1948, in the estate of the art dealer Bernhard A. Böhmer, who with three other dealers had been responsible for selling "degenerate" art abroad under National Socialism. Such a return was only possible in the Soviet Occupation Zone, however, where the military administration had issued the necessary order. In the west, the National Socialist law on confiscation from 1938 was not repealed. Many major works formerly in the Nationalgalerie are therefore now located in other museums worldwide. The losses could only be partially compensated for, at least in one case, however, spectacularly so: Kirchner's Berlin metropolitan scene *Rosa Strasse mit Auto* (Pink Street with Car, 1913), which since 1939 has belonged to the Museum of Modern Art in New York, could be replaced in 1999 by the large-format magnum opus of this series, *Potsdamer Platz* (1914).

After 1945, Ludwig Justi wanted to reconnect to the collection of modern art in the Kronprinzenpalais. Together with Adolf Jannasch, the head of the education department of the Magistrat of Greater Berlin, he developed the plan for a "gallery of the twentieth century."[4] In the early years, the focus of their acquisitions was on current art and works of

1 Neue Nationalgalerie, new hanging of the collection with works by Willi Sitte, Günther Uecker, and R. B. Kitaj, 1993–94

2 Nationalgalerie, modern department in the Kronprinzenpalais with Expressionist art, 1930

the prewar period. One of the most impressive purchases of this time was the large-format triptych *Nacht über Deutschland* (Night over Germany, 1945–46) by Horst Strempel, which illustrated the horrors of the war that had just ended. It was joined in the collection by, among other works, the wood sculpture *Das Paar* (The Couple, 1938) by Louise Stomps and paintings by Werner Heldt and Fritz Duda, all works of art from the 1930s that were still in the artists' galleries. In December 1947, the first painting from the early twentieth century followed: *Haus unter Bäumen* (House under Trees, 1910) by Karl Schmidt-Rottluff.

This path that initially had been taken jointly was cut off by the division of the city and the founding of the Federal Republic of Germany and the German Democratic Republic. The Nationalgalerie on the Museumsinsel (Museum Island) was located in the eastern part of the city. Justi continued to work there. Jannasch, by contrast, worked in the newly formed Magistrat of West Berlin. For the collection of the Nationalgalerie, which had been separated into East and West by the war, this resulted in distinct collection strategies, which from the outset were also political in character.

In the Soviet Occupation Zone, Walter Ulbricht, the future secretary general of the central committee of the Sozialistische Einheitspartei Deutschlands (Socialist Unity Party of Germany, SED), called for Socialist Realism in art based on the Soviet model.[5] This led to Justi in the East gradually abandoning the idea of a "gallery of the twentieth century" that he had initially still pursued. Although works of contemporary art that he had acquired in the first years after the war joined the holdings of the Nationalgalerie on the Museumsinsel, which was reopened in phases beginning in June 1949, they could not be shown under the increasingly restrictive art doctrine of the early 1950s. Not until December 1954, when the SED government had announced a new course in cultural policy after the death of Joseph Stalin, did Justi present, for the first time since the end of the Second World War, Expressionist and contemporary artworks, though he understood the latter to mean works by older artists such as Fritz Cremer, Otto Dix, Heinrich Ehmsen, Karl Hofer, and Otto Nagel.[6]

This could, however, scarcely have been called a "gallery of the twentieth century" (nor did it reflect a diversity associated with that name). There was, instead, a massive drive to found one in West Berlin from early 1949 onward. By 1954, Adolf Jannasch had acquired, as its director, more than 150 works of art. His collecting activities continued to focus on making amends to the artists who had been defamed as "degenerate" and on providing an account of the "living . . . connection of the art of our time to our culture as a whole," as Jannasch wrote.[7] In the early years, with the assistance of an acquisitions committee, Jannasch acquired works by the artists' groups Brücke (Bridge) and Blauer Reiter (Blue Rider) and by Max Beckmann, but also by international artists such as Fernand Léger and Piet Mondrian. From the younger generation, he purchased works by, among others, Hans Uhlmann, Ernst Wilhelm Nay, Willi Baumeister, and Henry Moore. In this way he sought to open up the collection to the art of the present day—from the West, it should be noted. At the end of 1954, the Galerie des 20. Jahrhunderts was given a permanent location in the former Landwehrcasino on Jebensstrasse right by Bahnhof Zoo. In the West Berlin of the postwar era, it was decidedly active and made considerable acquisitions. By contrast, for a long time the part of the Nationalgalerie that continued to operate in West Berlin had extremely limited funds available for acquisitions, so that only thirty-five works could be acquired in the entire decade of the 1950s.[8] The holdings of art, which had been moved to mines in the spring of 1945 to protect them from bombing, had first been secured by the American and British military authorities after the war and stored in Wiesbaden and Celle. This collection was shown in changing exhibitions beginning in the autumn of 1950 at Museum Dahlem and at Schloss Charlottenburg (Charlottenburg Palace, fig. 3). Their definitive return to West Berlin did not take place until 1957, with the founding of the Stiftung Preussischer Kulturbesitz (Prussian Cultural Heritage Foundation), to which the Staatliche Museen zu Berlin (National Museums in Berlin) also belong. As director general of the museums, Leopold Reidemeister had in fact already strongly advocated that the Galerie des 20. Jahrhunderts be merged with the Nationalgalerie.[9] The long-intended fusion did not take place, however, until 1967, shortly before the new museum building by Mies was completed.

Two National Galleries

The opening of the Neue Nationalgalerie on September 15, 1968, was a widely visible signal. Finally, West Berlin was able to present a prestigious museum and exhibition building and to assert itself in the field of art in competition with other museums in West Germany, but also in East Germany. In the spaces in the basement dedicated to the permanent collection, art from Romanticism to the present was shown. The glass hall was planned for changing exhibitions. In the East, by contrast, the original building of the Nationalgalerie was rededicated exclusively to the art of the nineteenth century in 1966, and the twentieth-century works were moved to the neighboring Altes Museum (Old Museum). The Sammlung der Kunst des 20. Jahrhunderts (Ost) (Collection of Twentieth-Century Art [East]) was not large at this point. Because funds were lacking and payments had to be made in East German deutschmarks, acquisitions could only happen within the GDR, which considerably limited the scope of the collection.[10] It was therefore primarily artists from the GDR—such as the sculptors Fritz Cremer, Waldemar Grzimek, Gustav Seitz—whose works entered the collection in the mid-1950s (fig. 4). Contemporary art was acquired more frequently only later, above all in the 1970s and 1980s, when under the political slogan "Weite und Vielfalt" (Breadth and Diversity) a broader spectrum of artistic themes and forms of stylistic expression could be considered (fig. 5). The art of the 1960s was represented by works by Willi Sitte, Wolfgang Mattheuer, and Werner Tübke; later years were represented by purchases from Manfred Böttcher (alias Strawalde), Arno Rink, and Walter Libuda. In the late 1960s, an effort was initiated to put together a collection of so-called proletarian-revolutionary—that is to say, political—art from the 1920s and 1930s, in an effort to establish a line of tradition from the artistic movements of the prewar era to art in the GDR. As a result, more and more works by Hans Grundig, Heinrich Ehmsen, Wilhelm Lachnit, and Otto Nagel entered the collection. Works leaning toward abstraction, such as those of Hermann Glöckner, remained an exception. Given the ideological conditions, artists largely had to stick to the figure and the object.[11] For that reason, the acquisitions do not include any positions that openly contradicted the politics of the GDR and do not document subversive alternative

3 Nationalgalerie (West), Constructivism room, Grosse Orangerie, Charlottenburg Palace, 1963

4 Nationalgalerie (East), room with contemporary art, works by sociocritical artists, 1954

5 Nationalgalerie (East), permanent exhibition of art from the German Democratic Republic, 1984

movements or international artists, not even from the socialist "fraternal countries" of Eastern Europe.

The West, by contrast, strove for internationality. This was evident not only in the choice of Mies van der Rohe as architect for the new museum building but also in the fact that Werner Haftmann, who was appointed the founding director of the Neue Nationalgalerie in 1967, spoke of a "gallery of the world," whereby in the context of the Cold War the "world" for him was limited to Western Europe and North America.[12] Haftmann had made a name for himself as author of the survey work *Malerei im 20. Jahrhundert* in 1954 (published in English translation in 1960 as *Painting in the Twentieth Century*) and as director of the first documenta in 1955. The view of twentieth-century art that he formulated there was to shape the understanding of art in West Germany for a long time and also to characterize his museum activity at the Neue Nationalgalerie. From 1968 onward, works of German art from Romanticism to the present were seen there in the context of European and international (Western) modernism. In consultation with Mies van der Rohe, the terrace was decorated by two large sculptures: one by the British artist Henry Moore and one by the American artist Alexander Calder.[13]

Even earlier, works by the likes of Ernst Wilhelm Nay and Marino Marini, and especially works from the circle of Art Informel, had entered in the collection. When Haftmann took over the position of director in 1967, he spoke of "modest holdings" and the need to fill gaps.[14] Consequently, he acquired first—to strengthen the Surrealism collection—a large-format work by Max Ernst, the painting *L'élue du mal* (The Elect of Evil) of 1928,[15] but his primary passion was postwar and contemporary art (fig. 6). Accordingly, he added to the collection works by Francis Bacon, R. B. Kitaj, Zoltán Kemény, and Tom Wesselmann. This trend continued under his successor, Dieter Honisch, who held that position from 1975 to 1997. He concentrated especially on American Color-Field painting, which he presented with works by Frank Stella, Ellsworth Kelly, and above all Barnett Newman's *Who's Afraid of Red, Yellow, and Blue IV* (1969–70) in the middle room of the floor for the permanent collection, which therefore was long known as the "American room" (fig. 7). At the same time, Honisch expanded the collection with works by the Gruppe ZERO of Düsseldorf and by other important West German artists such as Gotthard Graubner, Sigmar Polke, and Gerhard Richter.

Reunited

Following the reunification of both the two German states and the two national galleries, two decidedly distinct interpretations of the art of the twentieth century had to be merged. This was not so simple, as is evident from the controversy over the reorganization of the Neue Nationalgalerie in 1993–94, as discussed at the beginning of this essay.

It is this dual history of the collection, which in part also mirrored politics, that accounts for the quality and also the uniqueness of the merged holdings of twentieth-century art at the Neue Nationalgalerie. The collecting had occurred under the respective conditions of social and art policy of the German Reich, the Weimar Republic, National Socialism, and East and West Germany. During the division of Germany, the Nationalgalerie collections in the East and West had distinct profiles, both for the period after 1945 and for the era of Classical Modernism. Whereas in the West the tendency of the avant-garde to abstraction determined the perspective, in the East the figure and the object were principal. Whereas political art played an important role in the GDR, the internationality and the autonomy of art were emphasized in the Federal Republic.

Today, the collection includes more than 4,000 works of twentieth-century art. Gaps in the areas of Cubism and Surrealism, as well as in Pop, Minimal, and Conceptual Art, could be filled from the 1990s to the present by gifts and permanent loans from private collectors such as Heinz Berggruen, Julietta Scharf, Erich Marx, Friedrich Christian Flick, Egidio Marzona, and, most recently, Ulla and Heiner Pietzsch. Other tasks, such as incorporating non-European art and a greater focus on women artists, will continue to be important in the future.

The collection of the Nationalgalerie illustrates in a very special way the rifts and correspondences in art and history. It permits a contemporary look at and new reflection on the art of the twentieth century produced in Germany, Europe, and the United States.

1 Dieter Honisch, "Ein wichtiger Schritt zur Neuordnung der Sammlung des 20. Jahrhunderts in der Neuen Nationalgalerie," *Jahrbuch Preussischer Kulturbesitz* 30 (1993), pp. 75–85; Wolfgang Kahlcke, "Pressedokumentation zu einem durch die Neue Nationalgalerie ausgelösten 'deutschen Bilderstreit,'" *Jahrbuch Preussischer Kulturbesitz* 31 (1994), pp. 365–408.
2 See Udo Kittelmann et al., eds., *Die Sammlung der Nationalgalerie, 1945–1969: Der geteilte Himmel* (Berlin: Distanz Verlag, 2014).
3 See *Kunst in Deutschland, 1905–1937: Die verlorene Sammlung der Nationalgalerie im ehemaligen Kronprinzen-Palais; Dokumentation,* comp. Annegret Janda and Jörn Grabowski (Berlin: SMB, 1992).
4 See Maike Steinkamp, "Ein neues Kronprinzenpalais? Ludwig Justis Pläne für eine 'Galerie des 20. Jahrhunderts' nach 1945," *Jahrbuch der Berliner Museen* 52 (2010), supplement, *Ludwig Justi: Kunst und Öffentlichkeit*, pp. 117–21; Petra Winter, "Ein neues Kronprinzenpalais für Berlin: Der Weg zur Galerie des 20. Jahrhunderts 1945 bis 1948," in *Die Galerie des 20. Jahrhunderts in Berlin, 1945–1968: Der Weg zur Neuen Nationalgalerie,* ed. Christina Thomson and Petra Winter (Berlin: Deutscher Kunstverlag, 2015), pp. 14–45.
5 Walter Ulbricht, "Der Künstler im Zweijahresplan: Diskussionsrede auf der Arbeitstagung der Genossen Schriftsteller und Künstler," September 2, 1948, in *Zur Geschichte der deutschen Arbeiterbewegung: Aus Reden und Aufsätze,* vol. 3 ([East] Berlin: Dietz, 1963), pp. 312–16.
6 See Steinkamp, "Ein neues Kronprinzenpalais?," p. 121.
7 Adolf Jannasch, *Galerie des 20. Jahrhunderts* ([West] Berlin: Verwaltungsdruckerei, 1953), p. 3.
8 See Hanna Strzoda and Christina Thomson, "Wiederaufbau der Moderne: Die Galerie des 20. Jahrhunderts in West-Berlin 1949 bis 1968," in Thomson and Winter, *Die Galerie des 20. Jahrhunderts in Berlin, 1945–1968*, pp. 70–113, esp. pp. 96–97.
9 See ibid., p. 106.
10 See Vera Ruthenberg, "Hundert Jahre Sammlung der National-Galerie," in *Neuerwerbungen seit 1945: Jubiläums-Ausstellung zum hundertjährigen Bestehen der Sammlung 1861–1961,* exh. cat. Staatliche Museen zu Berlin ([East] Berlin: SMB, 1961), n.p.
11 See Eugen Blume and Roland März, "Re-Vision Kunst: Denkmäler und Sinnzeichen," in *Kunst in der DDR: Eine Retrospektive der Nationalgalerie,* ed. Fritz Jacobi, exh. cat. Neue Nationalgalerie, Berlin (Leipzig: E. A. Seemann, 2003), pp. 17–32, esp. p. 17.
12 See "Der Chef ist da!," *Der Abend,* February 25, 1967, p. 6, quoted in Christina Thomson, "Neubau und Fusion: Der Weg zur Neuen Nationalgalerie und den Vereinigten Kunstsammlungen 1961 bis 1968," in Thomson and Winter, *Die Galerie des 20. Jahrhunderts in Berlin, 1945–1968,* pp. 114–48, esp. p. 135.
13 See Joachim Jäger, *Neue Nationalgalerie Berlin: Mies van der Rohe* (Ostfildern: Hatje Cantz, 2011), p. 62.
14 See Werner Haftmann, "Von den Traditionen und vom Stand der Neuen Nationalgalerie," *Jahrbuch Preussischer Kulturbesitz* 5 (1967), pp. 169–85, esp. p. 182.
15 See *Nationalgalerie: Verzeichnis der vereinigten Kunstsammlungen, Nationalgalerie (Preussischer Kulturbesitz), Galerie des 20. Jahrhunderts* (Land Berlin) ([West] Berlin: SMB, 1968), p. 7.

6 Neue Nationalgalerie, presentation of the collection, 1974–75

7 Neue Nationalgalerie, presentation of the collection, *Räume des XX. Jahrhunderts*, room with American art, 2002–3

The Museum Operations

From Cloakrooms with Hat Racks to High-Performance Machine

Joachim Jäger, Constanze von Marlin

The Neue Nationalgalerie is the Neue Nationalgalerie is the Neue Nationalgalerie. But what does the name describe, really, a building or a use? Ludwig Mies van der Rohe had a completely free hand when designing the Berlin museum. In a postwar Germany heavily scarred by the Second World War, and in a Berlin then divided, the collection was still being rebuilt, so that no specific space allocation program imposed restrictions on the architect. The broad, spacious basement floor was designed for its collection, which at the time still included nineteenth-century art. The glass hall was intended for temporary exhibitions. As a "museum temple"—though also criticized in contemporaneous reviews as a "train station"—this hall was not always a celebrated exhibition venue. Had Mies created an extremely progressive museum building or dysfunctional architecture? The visionary design of a "stage for art" required two decades of curatorial practice, but also changes in the production of art, to unfold its diverse possibilities. The full potential of the now legendary hall developed only through the large formats in art from the 1980s onward, through artists increasingly thinking in terms of projects, and through a general tendency toward installation-based exhibitions. The spatial qualities of both levels—exhibition hall and basement—have, from today's perspective, proven themselves and even turned out to be especially forward-looking, precisely where the open character of the hall is concerned. The museum business has, however, changed over the years in such a way that not only the technology of the building but also its entire functionality reached the end of its useful life.

What has now happened with the refurbishment of the Neue Nationalgalerie is not just a restoration of the original idea of the building—a restoring of "as much Mies as possible," as David Chipperfield Architects formulated its motto. The restoration is also connected with a reset of the building, a reorientation of the museum's function and content, with an eye to a city of Berlin that has changed entirely since 1968, to a completely different social life, and also to an art world that has hardly anything to do with the situation of the 1960s. Precisely because the Neue Nationalgalerie represents not only significant architecture but was also deliberately designed by Mies van der Rohe as a functioning museum, historical preservation took the very operation of the museum into account in assessing the building's value as a historical landmark. The brief was not simply to reconstruct the architecture of Mies van der Rohe, but also to renovate the building so that it is suited to today's museum business. Naturally, changes to the Nationalgalerie itself also played a big role in that. The Neue Nationalgalerie has a completely different function today both in Berlin and within the Staatliche Museen zu Berlin (National Museums in Berlin) than the one it still had for West Berlin in 1968. Five large changes should be emphasized in particular.

The Collection

From 1968 to 1992, the Neue Nationalgalerie was an art museum of the City of West Berlin. Only part of today's collection belonged to this building. In particular, nineteenth-century art was also included in the collection (fig. 1). Major works by Caspar David Friedrich, Adolph von Menzel, and Max Liebermann shaped the identity of the institution, along with works of Western modernism. Until 1986, the collection of the Nationalgalerie (West) also included a collection of works on paper. Mies van der Rohe had planned the Grafisches Kabinett (Graphic Arts Gallery) on the basement floor for these works of art. Works on paper and prints could be viewed—as is common today in the reading rooms of large graphic arts institutions—in the original on sizeable study tables. This collection of drawings was transferred to the Kupferstichkabinett (Museum of Prints and Drawings) in 1986. Ever since, the Graphic Arts Gallery has functioned as a separate exhibition space rather than as an archive or storage room for works on paper.

The most far-reaching changes to the collection resulted, of course, from the fall of the Berlin Wall and from German reunification. The collections of the Nationalgalerie in the East and of the one in the West were combined; nineteenth century works were assigned to the Alte Nationalgalerie. The holdings in the East, including especially major works of Expressionism, came to the Neue Nationalgalerie in the West. Numerous donations, acquisitions, and long-term loans have been added since 1992. The current profile of the

1 Presentation of nineteenth-century art, 1969

2 Cloakroom in the exhibition hall, 1970

collection can by no means be compared any longer to the initial situation in 1968.[1]

The Institution

Back then, the Neue Nationalgalerie was "the" Nationalgalerie in the West. There was no other one in West Berlin, and the original building—the present Alte Nationalgalerie on the Museumsinsel (Museum Island)—was beyond its horizon, namely, in another political system, mentally and physically far removed from West Berlin. The "new" in Neue Nationalgalerie was therefore intended above all as a promise for the future, associated precisely with the idea of a "new art," that is, with a Western modernism oriented entirely toward innovation. Today, we would no longer describe it so unambiguously and emphatically. The "modernism" formulated by wealthy Western countries has also come to be criticized. In addition to questions of the "new," other themes of and attitudes toward art have been added. Moreover, six buildings now belong to the Nationalgalerie—and the planned new building at the Kulturforum (Cultural Forum) will soon make it seven. The focuses have been divided between them: the Alte Nationalgalerie and the Friedrichswerdersche Kirche (Friedrichswerder Church) are associated with nineteenth-century art; the Hamburger Bahnhof is responsible for the present day; two institutions in Charlottenburg are in turn special locations for Classical Modernism. One pursues a focus on Pablo Picasso and Paul Klee (Museum Berggruen) and the other the diversity of Surrealism (Scharf-Gerstenberg Collection). Much more so than before, the Neue Nationalgalerie takes on the function of a central platform for the art of the twentieth century. The major works of the combined collections of East and West can be seen here in changing presentations (from 2027, additional spaces will be available in the new building at the Kulturforum). Larger survey exhibitions on large art movements or individual artists can also be expected here. More than ever, the institution has a retrospective character. Its guiding idea is, to a large extent, the formative architecture of Mies, to which its visual communication also makes clear reference (fig. 6).

3 Light installation *Ba-O-Ba Berlin* by Keith Sonnier against the backdrop of Potsdamer Platz, 2002

Berlin

The city has, of course, transformed radically as well: the biotope of "West Berlin," with niches very much its own and almost anarchic opportunities, no longer exists. Architecturally, too, the situation has changed completely. Back then, in 1968, the Neue Nationalgalerie was built on the surreally empty site of what is now the Kulturforum, as only the second new building after the Philharmonie, designed by Hans Scharoun. From the terrace of the Neue Nationalgalerie, there was a broad view across what was then a vacant lot—a kind of no-man's-land—all the way to the Berlin Wall. Today, by contrast, the Neue Nationalgalerie has arrived in the center of the city. From here one can see the towers of Potsdamer Platz (fig. 3). Potsdamer Strasse itself is one of the highly trafficked, central urban axes of Berlin. This animated urban space makes its way into the building through large panes of glass, becoming part of the museum visually. This already signals one aspect: Berlin has a completely different role as compared to then; it is now the seat of the government and capital, a frequently visited travel destination, the largest university city in Germany, and also, of course, the capital of museums. The Neue Nationalgalerie is part of that, profiting from an agile urban society, which has meanwhile become very international, and also from tourism.

Indeed, it is associated above all with a very different volume of visitors than in the 1960s or 1970s. For example, for the 1976 exhibition *New York in Europa: Amerikanische Kunst aus europäischen Sammlungen* (New York in Europe: American Art from European Collections), 67,000 people came to the Neue Nationalgalerie, which at the time was an incredibly high number, because there were usually around 15,000 visitors to each exhibition. Nearly thirty years later, in 2004, *Das MoMA in Berlin* (MoMA in Berlin), attracted a record audience of more than a million people. The Gerhard Richter exhibition of 2012 was attended by 380,000 people. Even if these are extreme examples, admissions fluctuated around 300,000 annually. The cloakrooms, ticket counters (figs. 4, 5), and restrooms had not been designed for this vastly growing operation. For example, the only cloakrooms planned were the wooden built-ins in the exhibition hall (fig. 2). The hat rack reveals most clearly how much the architectural planning has aged today. Quite simply, space was lacking. Coatracks had to be setup temporarily at the bottom of the stairs, and later exhibition spaces were repurposed to provided adequate space for cloakrooms—a drastic measure that not only interrupted the path through the exhibition spaces that Mies had conceived but also posed a safety risk for fire protection.

As a result, part of the restoration concept of David Chipperfield Architects was to work out new solutions for several of the functional spaces. The two storerooms for art were moved outside, into a new building located under the terrace, to create two new public spaces in their former locations: a larger cloakroom and a spacious museum shop, which previously had been installed in the lower hall in a very improvised way. Both new spaces are recognizable as later additions as a result of an open and hence exposed, unfinished ceiling. In addition, an elevator for visitors has been integrated, almost invisibly, into one of the wooden cloakrooms in the hall. The food services offered in the café were simplified somewhat with a kind of self-service counter, giving more people the opportunity to take a coffee or lunch break. At the same time, in a collaboration with the Neue Nationalgalerie, the artist Jorge Pardo was invited to make the café more attractive, despite the lack of natural light, with an artistic design. Finally, new ticket desks, with room for the latest ticketing systems and media guides, replaced the original, very simple, square ticket counter that Mies had designed for the building.

Art Matters

Whereas in the 1960s, a distinction was made between the "permanent exhibition" (meaning the collection) and a few "special exhibitions," today's activities are characterized by a quasi explosion in art offerings of all kinds. Germany alone—in pandemic-free times—has an almost unmanageably broad diversity of exhibitions trying to draw attention through special advertising or symposia. The art itself, above all as a result of Conceptual Art and the temporally based arts of film and performance, is far removed from the ideas that Mies van der Rohe had imagined for this building. Special openings had to be designed to bring the large

4 Ticket desk and sales counter based on a design by Ludwig Mies van der Rohe, 1980s

5 Temporary museum shop for the exhibition *Französische Meisterwerke des 19. Jahrhunderts aus dem Metropolitan Museum of Art, New York* (French Masterpieces of the Nineteenth Century from the Metropolitan Museum of Art, New York), 2007

6 Poster in the new corporate design of the Neue Nationalgalerie, 2021

sculptures and other art into the hall. Above all, however, the conservation measures for the works have been fundamentally transformed. Today's art market, where twentieth-century art is especially highly valued, requires sharply higher insurance costs and guarantees, in order to be able to borrow and show works of art at all. Until now, the building has lacked climate control in the delivery areas for the conservational evaluation necessary for loans. Relocating a transformer station opened up space here that now provides a climate-controlled area for exhibition preparation. In other technical areas—such as the overall climate control of the building, lighting, and security options for works of art (alarms triggered by motion sensors in front of the pieces)—considerable and crucial improvements have been made in museum operations. Last but not least, the new storeroom for art created under the terrace now provides much safer, and at the same time much more easily accessible, storage of major works from the collection that are currently not on view.

Education

Art museums were long designed for an audience that was primarily bourgeois and well educated. The famous credo "Kultur für alle" (Culture for all) of Hilmar Hoffmann, who at the time was the cultural senator for Frankfurt am Main, launched a big offensive starting in the late 1970s for museum work to reach broader and more diverse sections of society. For decades now, educational activity has become increasingly important, especially with regard to special outreach proposals for circles or strata of the population that would otherwise not be considered classic museumgoers. In Berlin, which is a very complex, diverse city, this ambition has been tied to the challenge of taking this complexity and diversity more into account in the exhibition and educational program. For example, in today's museums there are, in addition to tours and audio guides, many other educational offerings aimed at a diverse audience, which have led to a separate educational room in the collection area of the Mies building—a place of exchange to invite visitors to become active themselves and work with or approach the content of the collection on site. At the same time, the importance of digital offerings is also growing. Naturally, a public Wi-Fi system has to be installed in the building. For the reopening of the Neue Nationalgalerie, a Mies website was developed to inform about its special architecture under the title "Neue Nationalgalerie Elements."

Despite all of these changes, the Neue Nationalgalerie remains the Neue Nationalgalerie. Many of these updating efforts have been integrated very discreetly into this landmark so as not to detract from the overall character of the building. With this reset of the museum, the Neue Nationalgalerie can once again adopt the role it had until it closed: being an important art museum aimed at a broad audience; stimulating diverse reflections and conversations with its exhibitions and collection presentations; and participating in current discourses through events and symposia. The name "Neue Nationalgalerie" represents a large venue for twentieth-century art with potential for further expansion. The new building at the Kulturforum, designed by the Swiss architects Herzog & de Meuron, will share that title and provide new spaces and opportunities for the art of the twentieth century. The history of the Neue Nationalgalerie will continue to be written.

1 For more detail on this, see the essay, "The Collection: Art of the Twentieth Century," by Maike Steinkamp and Dieter Scholz in the present volume, pp. 228–233.

DIREKTION

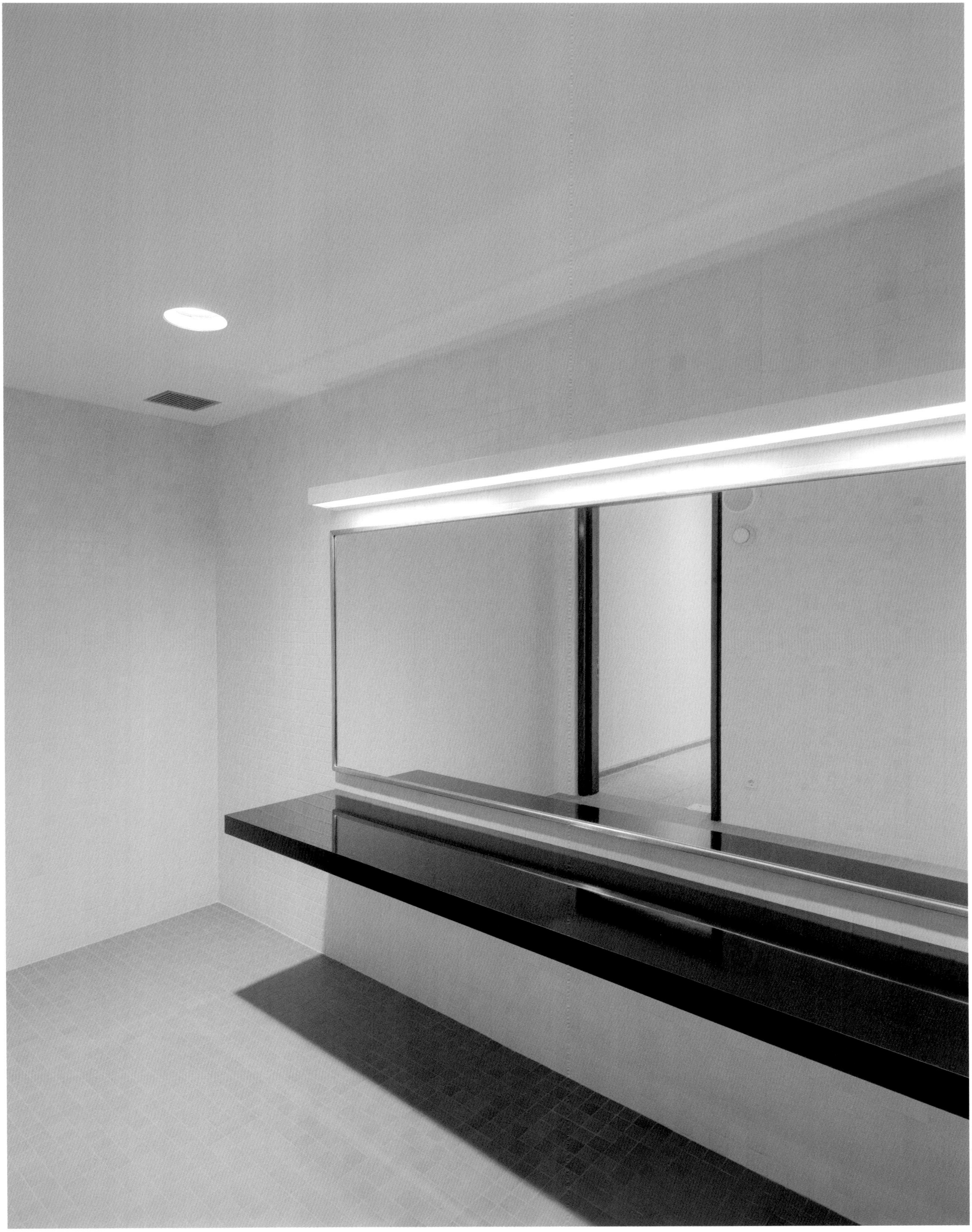

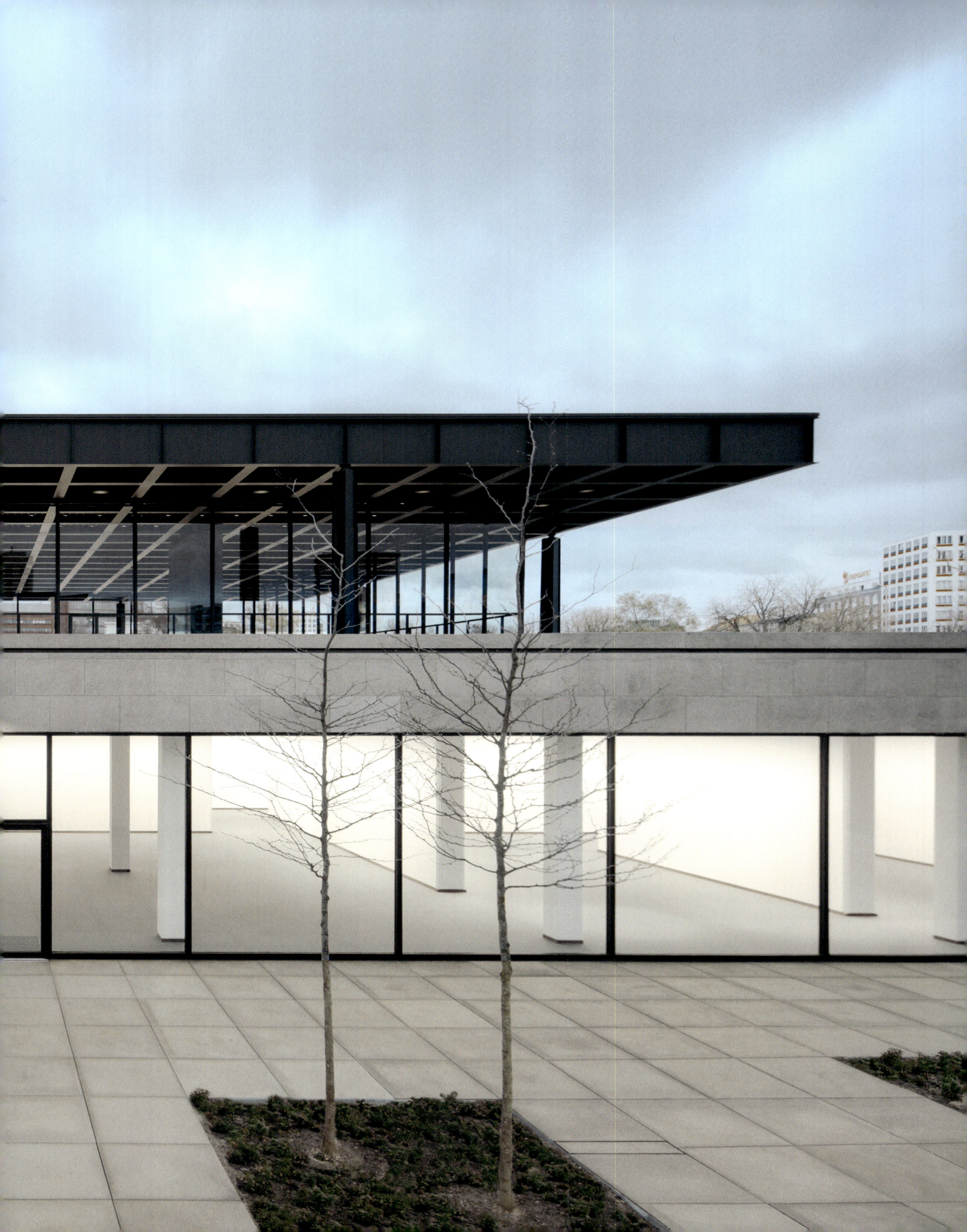

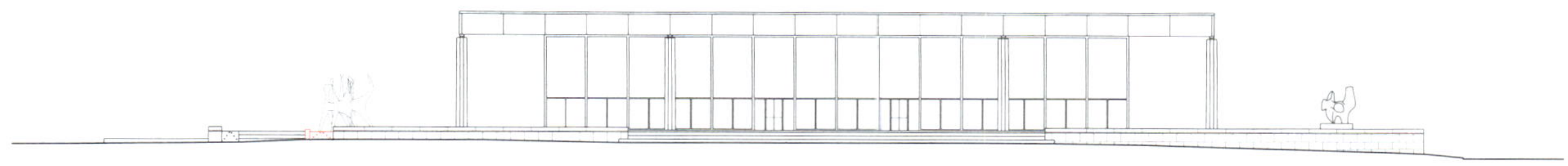

East view, historical and new

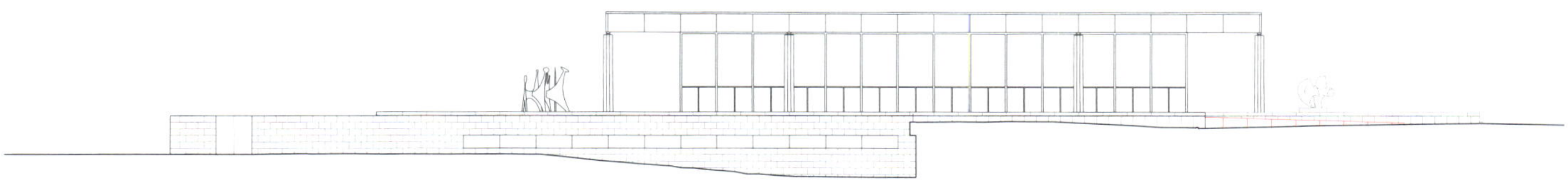

South view, historical and new

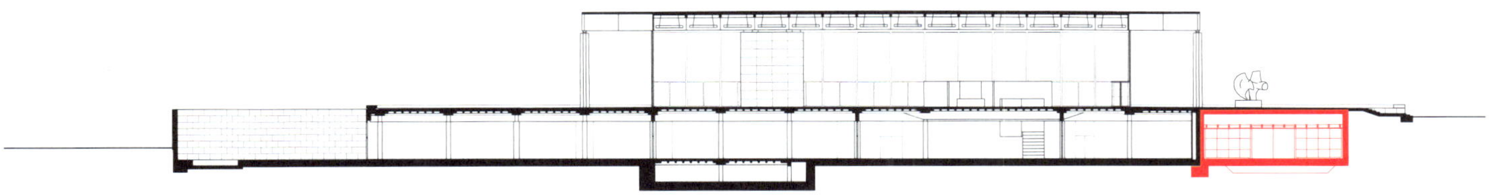

East–west sectional view, historical and new

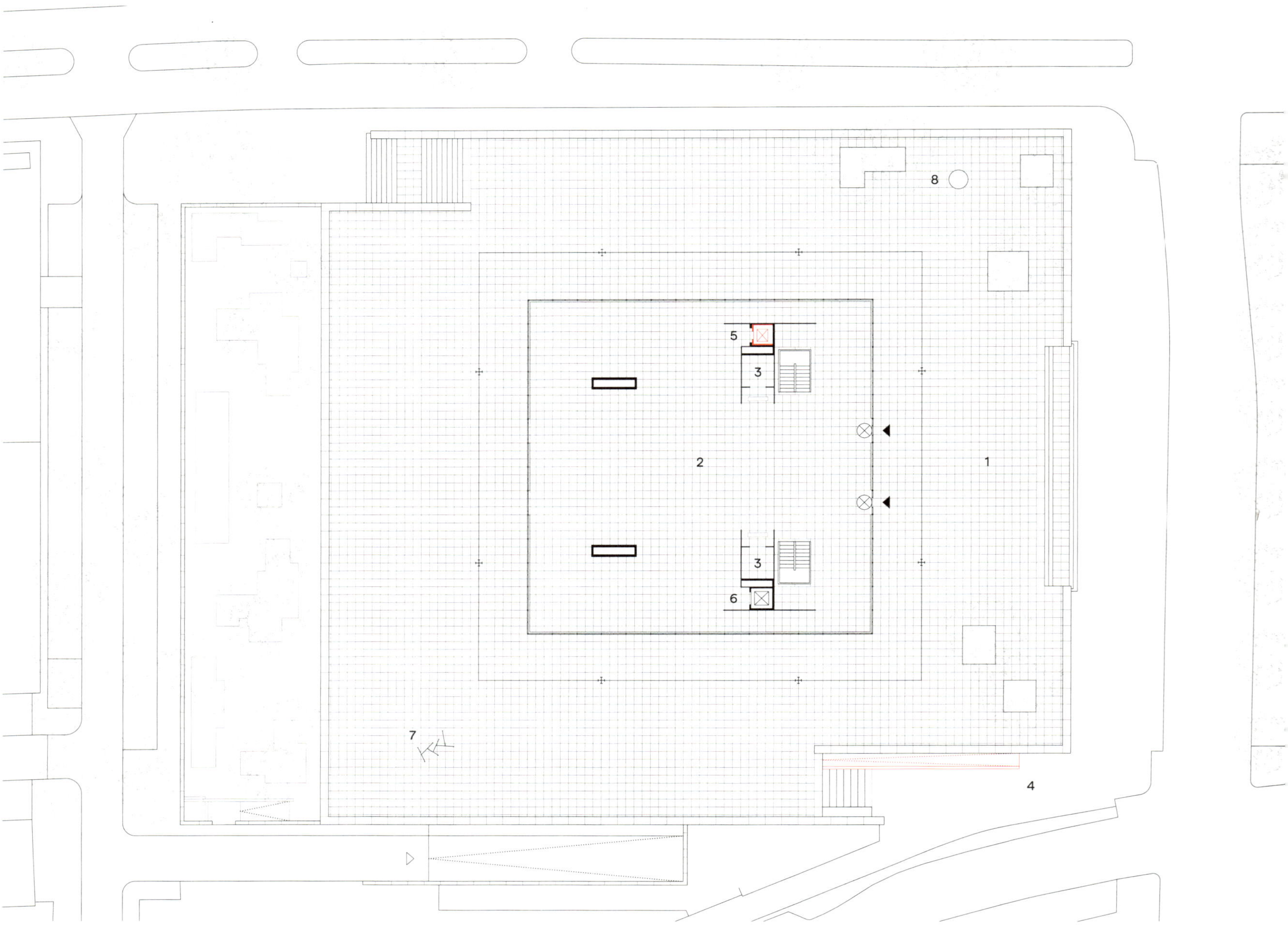

Ground floor plan, historical and new

1 Terrace
2 Exhibition hall
3 Cloakroom
4 New barrier-free access
5 New visitor elevator
6 Freight elevator
7 Sculpture *Têtes et Queue* by Alexander Calder, 1965
8 Sculpture *The Archer* by Henry Moore, 1964–65

Lower ground floor plan, historical and new

1 Stairway hall
2 Graphic Arts Gallery
3 Smaller exhibition hall
4 Grand exhibition hall
5 Sculpture garden
6 Museum shop in the former sculpture depot
7 Cloakroom in the former painting depot
8 Visitor restrooms
9 Café
10 Director's offices
11 Deliveries, service entrance
12 Exhibition preparation
13 Depot
14 Central ventilation room

Barry Bergdoll
is the Meyer Schapiro Professor of Art History at Columbia University and served as Chief Curator in the Department of Architecture and Design at the Museum of Modern Art, New York, from 2007 to 2014. He has curated various exhibitions including *Mies in Berlin* (2001, with Terry Riley), presented at MoMA, New York, and at Altes Museum, Berlin, and *Bauhaus 1919–1933: Workshops for Modernity* (2009). In addition to his work on Ludwig Mies van der Rohe, Bergdoll has written on Karl Friedrich Schinkel, Marcel Breuer, Frank Lloyd Wright, and on aspects of nineteenth-century French architecture.

David Chipperfield
studied architecture at the Kingston School of Art and the Architectural Association School of Architecture in London. In 1985, he founded David Chipperfield Architects, with offices in London, Berlin, Milan, and Shanghai. He has curated numerous exhibitions, including the 13th International Architecture Biennale in Venice (2012). In 2010, he received a knighthood for his services to architecture. For a lifetime's work, he was recognized with the RIBA Royal Gold Medal and the Praemium Imperiale. David Chipperfield has mentored the renovation of the Neue Nationalgalerie since 2012.

Beatriz Colomina
is the Howard Crosby Butler Professor of the History of Architecture at Princeton University. She writes and curates on questions of design, art, sexuality, and media. Her books include *Sexuality and Space* (1992), *Privacy and Publicity: Modern Architecture as Mass Media* (1994), *Domesticity at War* (2007), *Manifesto Architecture: The Ghost of Mies* (2014), *Clip/Stamp/Fold: The Radical Architecture of Little Magazines 196X to 197X* (2010), and *Are We Human? Notes on an Archaeology of Design* (2016). She has curated a number of exhibitions, including *Clip/Stamp/Fold* (2006), *Playboy Architecture* (2012), and *Radical Pedagogies* (2014). In 2016, she was co-curator of the 3rd Istanbul Design Biennial. Her latest book is *X-Ray Architecture* (2019).

Joachim Jäger
studied art history in Tübingen, Philadelphia, Munich, and Karlsruhe and wrote a dissertation on the artist Robert Rauschenberg. Since 2011, he has been the director of the Neue Nationalgalerie and curated numerous projects and exhibitions, including *Wolfgang Tillmans: Lighter* (2008), *Paul McCarthy: The Box* (2012), *Otto Piene: More Sky* (2014), and *Der Geteilte Himmel: Die Sammlung* (2014). Since 2012, Jäger has been involved in the renovation of the Neue Nationalgalerie; since 2015, he has also been responsible for planning the new building for the Nationalgalerie at the Kulturforum.

Phyllis Lambert
is Founding Director Emeritus of the Canadian Centre for Architecture in Montreal. She collaborated with Ludwig Mies van der Rohe and Philip Johnson on the Seagram Building, New York (completed in 1958), as chronicled in her 2013 book *Building Seagram*. She earned her Master of Architecture in 1963 from the Illinois Institute of Technology, Chicago. Lambert unswervingly works to advance democratic practices, contemporary architecture, and the social issues of urban conservation. She was awarded the Golden Lion for Lifetime Achievement at the 14th International Architecture Biennale in Venice (2014).

Christiane Lange
studied history and art history in Lausanne, Regensburg, and Bonn. She is a member of the working group Catalogue Raisonné of the Furniture and Furniture Designs of Ludwig Mies van der Rohe in Munich and the chairwoman of the Projekt MIK e. V. initiative. In recent years, she has conceived and realized research, exhibition, and film projects, including *Mies & Reich, Möbel & Räume*, Krefeld (2007), *MIES 1:1 Das Golfclub Projekt*, Krefeld (2010–13), and NRW's contribution to the Bauhaus centenary, *Bauhaus und Textilindustrie im Krefeld Pavillon von Thomas Schütte*, Krefeld (2015–19).

Dirk Lohan
architect, is a Fellow of the American Institute of Architects (FAIA). He studied at the Illinois Institute of Technology in Chicago and at the Technische Hochschule in Munich. In 1962, he worked in the firm of his grandfather Ludwig Mies van der Rohe and was responsible for building the Neue Nationalgalerie in Berlin. From 1975 to 2019, he was the director of various architectural firms under his name. In recognition of his many prizewinning buildings, Lohan was elected fellow of the AIA. As of 2020, he is the founder and head architect of Lohan Architecture LLC in Chicago.

Constanze von Marlin
studied art history in Berlin and Amsterdam. Her dissertation, *Public Art: Zum Öffentlichkeitscharakter der Minimal Art*, was published in 2007. As a curator, she has worked at the Hochschule für Bildende Künste in Dresden and the Kunstverein Junge Kunst in Wolfsburg. She has published numerous contributions on art and on art in public space. In 2011, she cofounded the firm schmedding.vonmarlin. with a focus on art and architecture projects.

Simon Menges
While studying architecture, he moved to Shanghai and took on his first assignments for David Chipperfield Architects. In parallel with his three-year studio assistantship for Wolfgang Tillmans, he began to document the built environment. Since then he has been photographing in an architectural context internationally.

Fritz Neumeyer
is an architect with a doctorate of engineering. He was professor of architecture theory at the Technische Universität in Berlin from 1993 to 2012. In 1992, he was the Jean Labatut Professor at Princeton University. From 1989 to 1992, he was professor of architecture history at the Universität Dortmund. His many publications include *Mies van der Rohe: Das kunstlose Wort* (Berlin, 1986), translated as *The Artless Word* (Cambridge, MA, 1991), also translated into Spanish, French, and Italian in 1996, Korean in 2009, and Chinese in 2020, and reissued in Berlin in 2016.

Martin Reichert
studied art history and classical archaeology in Berlin and Vienna, and architecture at the Technische Universität in Berlin. He has been active as an architect since 1993, first with Gerhard Spangenberg, then from 2000 with David Chipperfield Architects in Berlin; since 2011, one of the managing directors and partners, with a focus on cultural buildings and landmark conservation. Since 2012, the partner responsible for the renovation of the Neue Nationalgalerie.

Manfredo di Robilant
is an architect. He served as a research associate for the 14th International Architecture Biennale in Venice (2014), for which he designed the main entrance installation and authored two books. He was a visiting scholar at CCA Montréal after postdoctoral work at the Politecnico di Torino, from which he holds a PhD in the history of modern architecture. In 2012, he co-founded the architectural firm DAR architettura with Giovanni Durbiano and Alessandro Armando.

Dieter Scholz
studied art history and and sociology in Tübingen and Hamburg, receiving his MA in 1988 and his PhD in 1994. From 1995 to 1999, he was an intern and worked on contract for the Staatliche Museen zu Berlin; from 1999 to 2003, he was an advisor to the director general at the museum kunstpalast in Düsseldorf. Since 2003 has been a curator for the art of classical modernism at the Neue Nationalgalerie in Berlin (until 2009 he was also responsible for the Museum Berggruen and Sammlung Scharf-Gerstenberg). His exhibitions include *Die schwarzen Jahre* (2015) and *Rudolf Belling* (2017).

Erik Spiekermann
is a graphic designer. His work has been a distinctive part of the visual world since the 1970s. As the founder of MetaDesign and Edenspiekermann, he created an unmistakable look for the BVG Berlin, the Deutsche Bahn, the *Economist*, and brands such as Audi, VW, and Bosch, among others. FontShop, the first mail-order company for computer fonts, was his idea; and his type designs, including ITC Officina and FF Meta, are familiar to every designer. Spiekermann remains a central figure of the German and international design scene. He runs a typographic workshop in Berlin with the motto "Hacking Gutenberg."

Maike Steinkamp
studied art history and German and Romance literature in Bonn and Parma. She received her doctorate in 2007. From 2001 to 2004, she worked at the Kunst- und Ausstellungshalle Bonn and the Deutsches Historisches Museum, then as a research associate at the Kunstgeschichtliches Seminar of the Universität Hamburg. In 2009, she was a visiting professor at Smith College, Northampton, MA. From 2012 to 2017 she was curator of the Stiftung Arp e. V., Berlin/Rolandswerth. Since 2018, she has been a curator at the Neue Nationalgalerie.

Wolf Tegethoff
studied art history, urban design, and economic, social, and constitutional history in Bonn and at Columbia University in New York. After receiving his doctorate in 1981, he was an assistant professor at the Universität Kiel. In 1987, he transferred to the Zentralinstitut für Kunstgeschichte in Munich, where he was director for three decades as of 1989. He is an honorary professor at the Universität München. Since 2018, he has lived and taught in Dresden. His research focuses on the architecture and furniture design of the nineteenth and twentieth centuries, with many publications on the work of Ludwig Mies van der Rohe in particular.

Claire Zimmerman
studied architecture and history in Philadelphia, Cambridge, MA, and New York. She wrote her dissertation on Ludwig Mies van der Rohe and photography. Since 2013 she has been an associate professor at the University of Michigan in Ann Arbor. She has authored the books *Photographic Architecture in the Twentieth Century* (2014) and *Mies van der Rohe* (2006); and she co-edited with Mark Crinson the publication *Neo-Avant-Garde and Postmodern: Postwar Architecture in Britain and Beyond* (2010). She has been involved in curatorial projects at Tate Britain in London (*New Brutalist Image*) and in Ann Arbor, as well as in research on *Mies in Berlin* (MoMA) and *James Frazer Stirling* (CCA/Yale Center for British Art).

Cover: Staatliche Museen zu Berlin/Simon Menges
p. 2: Landesarchiv Berlin, F Rep. 290 (05) No. 0119286/Ludwig Ehlers
pp. 9–32: Staatliche Museen zu Berlin/Simon Menges
p. 34, 1: Ludwig Mies van der Rohe: Riehl House. Potsdam-Neubabelsberg, Germany, 1906–07. Photograph William & Meyer Co., Chicago. Mies van der Rohe Archive, gift of the architect. Acc. no.: MI144. © 2021. Digital image, The Museum of Modern Art, New York/Scala, Florence
p. 34, 2: bpk/Kupferstichkabinett, Staatliche Museen zu Berlin/Jörg P. Anders
p. 35, 3: bpk/Kupferstichkabinett, Staatliche Museen zu Berlin/Volker-H. Schneider
p. 37, 4: Ludwig Mies van der Rohe: Museum for a Small City project, 1941–43. Pencil, ink, plastic film, airbrush on Gelatin silver print, 8 × 10 in. (20.3 × 25.4 cm). Mies van der Rohe Archive, gift of the architect. Acc. no.: MR4201.1. © 2021. Digital image, The Museum of Modern Art, New York/Scala, Florence
p. 37, 5: bpk/Kupferstichkabinett, Staatliche Museen zu Berlin/Wolfram Büttner
p. 38, 6: Library of Congress, Prints & Photographs Division, Balthazar Korab Collection, reproduction number LC-DIG-ds-11546
p. 41, 7: Staatliche Museen zu Berlin/Zentralarchiv/Reinhard Friedrich, art: Wilhelm Lehmbruck
p. 43, 8: Staatliche Museen zu Berlin/Zentralarchiv/Reinhard Friedrich
pp. 44–45: Landesarchiv Berlin, F Rep. 290 (02) No. 0018224/Bert Sass
pp. 46–47: Landesarchiv Berlin, F Rep. 290 (05) No. 0112680/Johann Willa
p. 48: Staatliche Museen zu Berlin/Zentralarchiv/Reinhard Friedrich
p. 49: Landesarchiv Berlin, F Rep. 290 (05) No. 0115550/Johann Willa
p. 50: Heinz Oeter
p. 51 top: Heinz Oeter, bottom: Staatliche Museen zu Berlin/Zentralarchiv/Reinhard Friedrich
p. 52: Landesarchiv Berlin, F Rep. 290 (05) No. 0119381/Ludwig Ehlers
p. 53: Landesarchiv Berlin, F Rep. 290 (05) No. 0119385/Ludwig Ehlers
pp. 54–55: Manfred Niermann (CC BY-SA 4.0)
p. 56: bpk/Kunstbibliothek, SMB/Dietmar Katz
p. 57: bpk/Kunstbibliothek, SMB/Dietmar Katz
p. 58, 1: Library of Congress, Prints & Photographs Division, Balthazar Korab Collection, reproduction number LC-DIG-ds-11538
p. 58, 2: HB-21253-B, Chicago History Museum, Hedrich-Blessing Collection
p. 59, 3: HB-13809-J5, Chicago History Museum, Hedrich-Blessing Collection
p. 60, 4: Staatliche Museen zu Berlin/Neue Nationalgalerie/David L. Hirsch
p. 62, 5: Staatliche Museen zu Berlin/Zentralarchiv/Reinhard Friedrich, art: Piet Mondrian
p. 62, 6 top: Landesarchiv Berlin, F Rep. 290 (05) No. 0119282/Ludwig Ehlers, bottom: Landesarchiv Berlin, F Rep. 290 (05) No. 0119285/Ludwig Ehlers
pp. 64–65: Staatliche Museen zu Berlin/Zentralarchiv/Reinhard Friedrich
p. 66: Staatliche Museen zu Berlin/Zentralarchiv/Reinhard Friedrich
p. 67 top and bottom: Staatliche Museen zu Berlin/Zentralarchiv/Reinhard Friedrich
pp. 68–69: Library of Congress, Prints & Photographs Division, Balthazar Korab Collection, reproduction number LC-DIG-ds-11551, art: Piet Mondrian
p. 70: Staatliche Museen zu Berlin/Zentralarchiv/Reinhard Friedrich
p. 71: Staatliche Museen zu Berlin/Neue Nationalgalerie/Reinhard Friedrich, art: Gerhard Marcks, VG Bild-Kunst, Bonn, 2021
p. 72: Staatliche Museen zu Berlin/Zentralarchiv/Reinhard Friedrich, art: Henry Moore
p. 73: Staatliche Museen zu Berlin/Zentralarchiv/Reinhard Friedrich, art: Alexander Calder
pp. 74–75: Staatliche Museen zu Berlin/Zentralarchiv/Reinhard Friedrich
pp. 76–77: Stadtmuseum Berlin/Ludwig Binder, reproduction: Matthias Viertel, Berlin, art: Kenneth Snelson
pp. 78–79: Staatliche Museen zu Berlin/Neue Nationalgalerie/Reinhard Friedrich, art: François Morellet, VG Bild-Kunst, Bonn, 2021
p. 81, 1: Klaus Israel
p. 82, 2: Ludwig Mies van der Rohe: Resor House, project (Jackson Hole, Wyoming), 1937–41 (unbuilt). Graphite and collage of wood veneer and cut-and-pasted reproduction and photograph and graphite on illustration board, 30 × 40 in. (76.1 × 101.5 cm). Mies van der Rohe Archive, gift of the architect. Acc. no.: 716.1963. © 2021. Digital image, The Museum of Modern Art, New York/Scala, Florence, art: Paul Klee
p. 82, 3: Ludwig Mies van der Rohe: Museum for a Small City, project, 1942. Cut-out photographs and photographic reproductions on illustration board, 30 × 40 in. (76.2 × 101.6 cm). Mies van der Rohe Archive, gift of the architect. Acc. no.: 724.1963. © 2021. Digital image, The Museum of Modern Art, New York/Scala, Florence, art: Pablo Picasso, Succession Picasso, VG Bild-Kunst, Bonn, 2021, Aristide Maillol
p. 85, 4: bpk/Staatliche Museen zu Berlin/Nationalgalerie/Jörg P. Anders, art: Wassily Kandinsky, Wilhelm Lehmbruck
p. 86, 5: Staatliche Museen zu Berlin/Neue Nationalgalerie/Reinhard Friedrich
p. 91, 1: Robert Gerhardt. Gelatin silver print, 4 × 4 in. (10.2 × 10.2 cm). Mies van der Rohe Archive, gift of the architect. No. MMA14216. © 2021. Digital image, The Museum of Modern Art, New York/Scala, Florence
p. 92, 2: William Leftwich, Edward A. Duckett Sammlung, Ryerson and Burnham Art and Architecture, The Art Institute of Chicago, Bildnummer 198602.081216-03
p. 92, 3: Stadtmuseum Berlin/Ludwig Binder, reproduction: Matthias Viertel, Berlin, art: Piet Mondrian
p. 93, 4: Staatliche Museen zu Berlin/Zentralarchiv/Reinhard Friedrich
p. 93, 5: Staatliche Museen zu Berlin/Neue Nationalgalerie/Reinhard Friedrich
p. 94, 6: Staatliche Museen zu Berlin/Zentralarchiv/Reinhard Friedrich
p. 95, 7 top and bottom: Staatliche Museen zu Berlin/Zentralarchiv/Reinhard Friedrich, art: Wilhelm Lehmbruck
p. 96, 8: Ludwig Mies van der Rohe, Lilly Reich: Die Wohnung (The Dwelling), Deutsche Werkbund Exhibition, Stuttgart, Germany, 1927. Gelatin silver print, 6 5/8 × 9 in. (16.8 × 22.9 cm). Mies van der Rohe Archive, gift of the architect. No. MMA16.806. © 2021. Digital image, The Museum of Modern Art, New York/Scala, Florence
p. 96, 9: Archivo ABC, Barcelona
p. 97, 10: Klassik Stiftung Weimar, Bauhaus-Museum, acquisition from private ownership, art: Georg Kolbe
p. 97, 11: Ludwig Mies van der Rohe: Tugendhat House, Brno, Czech Republic, 1930. Gelatin silver print, 8 × 10 in. (20.3 × 25.4 cm). Mies van der Rohe Archive, gift of the architect. Acc. no.: AD624. © 2021. Digital image, The Museum of Modern Art, New York/Scala, Florence
p. 98, 12: Library of Congress, Prints & Photographs Division, photograph by Carol M. Highsmith, reproduction number LC-DIG-highsm-13100
p. 98, 13: Werner Blaser, Blaser Architekten
p. 99, 14: Ludwig Mies van der Rohe: Resor House, Jackson Hole, Wyoming (USA), 1937–38. 20 × 30 in. (50.8 × 76.2 cm). Mies van der Rohe Archive, gift of the architect. No. MR3800.808. © 2021. Digital image, The Museum of Modern Art, New York/Scala, Florence
p. 102, 1: Ludwig Mies van der Rohe: Project for Concert Hall, 1942. Graphite, cut-and-pasted photo reproduction, cut-and-pasted papers, cut-and-pasted painted paper, and gouache on Gelatin silver photograph mounted on board, 29 1/2 × 62 in. (75 × 157.5 cm). Mies van der Rohe Archive, gift of Mrs. Mary Callery. No. 571.1963. © 2021. Digital image, The Museum of Modern Art, New York/Scala, Florence
p. 103, 2: Library of Congress, Prints & Photographs Division, Balthazar Korab Collection, reproduction number LC-DIG-ppem-00695
p. 104, 3 top and bottom: Staatliche Museen zu Berlin/Zentralarchiv/Reinhard Friedrich, art: Franz Erhard Walther, VG Bild-Kunst, Bonn, 2021
p. 105, 4: Ludwig Mies van der Rohe: Neue Nationalgalerie, Gallery of 20th Century, preliminary version, section. Pencil and ink on acetate, 36 1/2 × 63 1/2 in. (92.7 × 161.3 cm). Mies van der Rohe Archive, gift of the architect. No. MR6204.12. © 2021. Digital image, The Museum of Modern Art, New York/Scala, Florence
p. 107, 5: Ivo Faber, VG Bild-Kunst, Bonn, 2021, art: Imi Knoebel, VG Bild-Kunst, Bonn, 2021
p. 108, 6: Mila Hacke, art: Rudolf Stingel
p. 110, 7: Staatliche Museen zu Berlin/Neue Nationalgalerie/Simon Vogel, art: Duane Hanson, VG Bild-Kunst, Bonn, 2021, Willi Sitte, VG Bild-Kunst, Bonn, 2021
p. 110, 8: Staatliche Museen zu Berlin/Neue Nationalgalerie/Werner Zellien, VG Bild-Kunst, Bonn, 2021, art: Barnett Newman, Barnett Newman Foundation, VG Bild-Kunst, Bonn, 2021
pp. 113–36: Staatliche Museen zu Berlin/Simon Menges
p. 139, 1: Otto Borutta, reproduction: Anja Elisabeth Witte/Berlinische Galerie
p. 139, 2: Otto Borutta, reproduction: Anja Elisabeth Witte/Berlinische Galerie
p. 140, 3: Albert Kahn Associates records, Bentley Historical Library, University of Michigan
p. 140, 4: Architectural Forum, Nov. 1941
p. 140, 5: United States Army Air Forces, USGOV-PD
p. 141, 6: Ludwig Mies van der Rohe: Convention Hall. Chicago, Illinois, 1953. Marbleized paper, cut-out photographs (of roof-truss model and 1952 Republican Party Convention) on composition board, 33 × 48 in. (83.9 × 122 cm). Mies van der Rohe Archive, gift of the architect. No. 572.1963. © 2021. Digital image, The Museum of Modern Art, New York/Scala, Florence
p. 144, 1: Ludwig Mies van der Rohe: Kroeller Mueller Project, Wassenaar (The Netherlands), 1912. Gelatin silver print, 5 3/4 × 9 1/2 in. (14.6 × 24.1 cm). Mies van der Rohe Archive, gift of the architect. No. MMA17.137. © 2021. Digital image, The Museum of Modern Art, New York/Scala, Florence

p. 145, 2: Staatliche Museen zu Berlin/Zentralarchiv/Reinhard Friedrich, art: Gerhard Marcks, VG Bild-Kunst, Bonn, 2021
p. 146, 3: Ludwig Mies van der Rohe: Exhibition House, German Building Exhibition, Berlin, 1930–31. Gelatin silver photograph, 6 5/8 × 9 in. (16.8 × 22.9 cm). Mies van der Rohe Archive, gift of the architect. No. MMA 1939. © 2021. Digital image, The Museum of Modern Art, New York/Scala, Florence
p. 146, 4: Ludwig Mies van der Rohe: Exhibition House, German Building Exhibition, Berlin, Germany (Plan), 1930–31. Ink on illustration board, 30 × 40 in. (76.2 × 101.6 cm). Mies van der Rohe Archive, gift of the architect. No. MR25.237. © 2021. Digital image, The Museum of Modern Art, New York/Scala, Florence
p. 149, 5: The Museum of Modern Art Archives, NY. PA245. © 2021. Digital image, The Museum of Modern Art, New York/Scala, Florence
p. 149, 6: Mies van der Rohe Archive, The Museum of Modern Art, New York
p. 150, 7: Bauhaus-Archiv Berlin
p. 153, 8: Landesarchiv Berlin, F Rep. 290 (05) No. 0181342/Karl-Heinz Schubert
p. 155, 1 top: Heinz Oeter, bottom: BBR/Marcus Ebener
p. 156, 2: bpk
p. 156, 3: Ludwig Mies van der Rohe: Bismarck Monument Project, Bingen, Germany, 1910. Gouache on canvas, 55 1/2 × 7 10 1/2 in. (141 × 240 cm). Robert Beyer Purchase Fund, Edward Larrabee Barnes Purchase Fund, Marcel Breuer Purchase Fund, and Philip Johnson Purchase Fund. No. 192.1998. © 2021. Digital image, The Museum of Modern Art, New York/Scala, Florence
p. 156, 4: HB-17378-D, Chicago History Museum, Hedrich-Blessing Collection
p. 157, 5: HB-37936-B, Chicago History Museum, Hedrich-Blessing Collection
p. 158, 6: Staatliche Museen zu Berlin/Neue Nationalgalerie/Reinhard Friedrich
p. 161, 7: Ute Zscharnt for David Chipperfield Architects
p. 163, 1: Ludwig Mies van der Rohe: 50 × 50 House, presentation plan, 1951–52. Mies van der Rohe Archive, gift of the architect. No. MR5016.103. © 2021. Digital image, The Museum of Modern Art, New York/Scala, Florence
p. 164, 2: HB-25151-E, Chicago History Museum, Hedrich-Blessing Collection
p. 164, 3: BBR/Thomas Bruns
p. 166, 4: bpk/Nationalgalerie im Hamburger Bahnhof, SMB, Sammlung Marx/Jochen Littkemann, art: Donald Judd, Judd Foundation, VG Bild-Kunst, Bonn, 2021
p. 167, 5: John Cage: Music for Carillon, # 4, Page 3, 1961. Ink on transparentized graph paper, 11 × 16 5/8 in. (28 × 42.3 cm), mount 12 1/8 × 17 1/8 in. (30.9 × 43.5 cm). Acquired with matching funds from Gertrud A. Mellon and the National Endowment for the Arts. No. 5.1977. © 2021. Digital image, The Museum of Modern Art, New York/Scala, Florence
pp. 169–92: Staatliche Museen zu Berlin/Simon Menges
p. 194, 1: Mies van der Rohe Archive, The Museum of Modern Art, New York
p. 194, 2: Collection H. J. Lange, Ammersbek
p. 195, 3: Staatliche Museen zu Berlin/Zentralarchiv/Reinhard Friedrich
p. 195, 4: Ludwig Mies van der Rohe: Neue Nationalgalerie, Berlin, Germany, ca. 1962–68. Photomontage with marbelized paper, wood veneer. 39.4 × 106 cm. Mies van der Rohe Archive, gift of the architect. No. MR6204.49. © 2021. Digital image, The Museum of Modern Art, New York/Scala, Florence
pp. 196–97, 5–8: Carsten Krohn
p. 199, 9: Staatliche Museen zu Berlin/Zentralarchiv/Reinhard Friedrich
p. 199, 10: Staatliche Museen zu Berlin/Neue Nationalgalerie/Reinhard Friedrich, art: Wilhelm Lehmbruck
p. 200, 11: Carsten Krohn
p. 201, 12: Akademie der Künste (AdK), Berlin, Reinhard-Friedrich-Archiv 474, Photo 168
p. 201, 13: Staatliche Museen zu Berlin/Zentralarchiv/Reinhard Friedrich
p. 202, 14: bpk/Staatliche Museen zu Berlin/Nationalgalerie/Jörg P. Anders, art: Pablo Picasso, Succession Picasso, VG Bild-Kunst, Bonn, 2021, Wilhelm Lehmbruck, Auguste Renoirs
p. 205, 1: Staatliche Museen zu Berlin/Zentralarchiv/Reinhard Friedrich
p. 206, 2: photographer unknown
p. 206, 3: Ute Zscharnt for David Chipperfield Architects
p. 207, 4: Landesarchiv Berlin, F Rep. 290 (05) No. 0136591/Odehnal, art: Wilhelm Lehmbruck
p. 208, 5: HB-27889-G, Chicago History Museum, Hedrich-Blessing Collection
p. 208, 6: BBR/Thomas Bruns
p. 210, 7: BBR/Marcus Ebener
p. 210, 8: Archiv Daniela Hammer-Tugendhat
p. 210, 9: Staatliche Museen zu Berlin/Zentralarchiv/Reinhard Friedrich
p. 214, 5: Staatliche Museen zu Berlin/Kunstbibliothek/Dietmar Katz
p. 215, 6 top: BBR/Thomas Bruns, bottom: Staatliche Museen zu Berlin/Simon Menges
pp. 216–27: Ute Zscharnt for David Chipperfield Architects, except p. 219 top: Christian Martin
p. 229, 1: Staatliche Museen zu Berlin/Zentralarchiv/Reinhard Friedrich, art: Willi Sitte, VG Bild-Kunst, Bonn, 2021, Günther Uecker, VG Bild-Kunst, Bonn, 2021, Ronald B. Kitaj, R.B. Kitaj Estate
p. 229, 2: Staatliche Museen zu Berlin, Zentralarchiv, art: Edwin Scharff, VG Bild-Kunst, Bonn, 2021, August Macke, Franz Marc, Heinrich Nauen, Paul Adolf Seehaus
p. 231, 3: Staatliche Museen zu Berlin, Nationalgalerie, Walter Steinkopf, art: Jean Arp, VG Bild-Kunst, Bonn, 2021, Hans Uhlmann, VG Bild-Kunst, Bonn, 2021, Henryk Berlewi, László Moholy-Nagy
p. 231, 4: Staatliche Museen zu Berlin, Zentralarchiv, art: Josef Hegenbarth, VG Bild-Kunst, Bonn, 2021, Otto Nagel, VG Bild-Kunst, Bonn, 2021, Heinrich Ehmsen, Gustav Seitz
p. 231, 5: Staatliche Museen zu Berlin, Zentralarchiv, Rosa Mai, art: Fritz Duda, VG Bild-Kunst, Bonn, 2021, Harald Metzkes, VG Bild-Kunst, Bonn, 2021, Waldemar Grizmek
p. 233, 6: Staatliche Museen zu Berlin/Zentralarchiv/Reinhard Friedrich, art: Henry Moore, reproduced by permission of The Henry Moore Foundation, Max Ernst, VG Bild-Kunst, Bonn, 2021, Constantin Brancusi, Succession Brancusi – All rights reserved, VG Bild-Kunst, Bonn, 2021, Sam Francis, Sam Francis Foundation, California, VG Bild-Kunst, Bonn, 2021, Naum Gabo, The Work of Naum Gabo © Nina & Graham Williams/Tate
p. 233, 7: Staatliche Museen zu Berlin/Neue Nationalgalerie/Roman März, art: Sol LeWitt, VG Bild-Kunst, Bonn, 2021, Frank Stella, VG Bild-Kunst, Bonn, 2021
p. 235, 1: Staatliche Museen zu Berlin/Neue Nationalgalerie/Reinhard Friedrich, art: Caspar David Friedrich
p. 235, 2: Stadtmuseum Berlin/Ludwig Binder, reproduction: Matthias Viertel, Berlin
p. 236, 3: Staatliche Museen zu Berlin/Christian Gahl, art: Keith Sonnier, VG Bild-Kunst, Bonn, 2021
p. 238, 4: Staatliche Museen zu Berlin/Zentralarchiv/Reinhard Friedrich
p. 238, 5: David von Becker
p. 239, 6: Staatliche Museen zu Berlin/Neue Nationalgalerie, art: Christian Schad, Christian Schad Stiftung Aschaffenburg, VG Bild-Kunst, Bonn, 2021
pp. 241–64: Staatliche Museen zu Berlin/Simon Menges, art p. 254: Marina Nuñez del Prado, p. 256: Bernhard Heiliger, VG Bild-Kunst, Bonn, 2021, Ernesto de Fiori, p. 259: Bernhard Luginbühl, Wilhelm Loth
pp. 265–67: David Chipperfield Architects
Ludwig Mies van der Rohe, VG Bild-Kunst, Bonn, 2021

For the Nationalgalerie,
Staatliche Museen zu Berlin,
edited by Joachim Jäger
and Constanze von Marlin

Concept:
Joachim Jäger,
Constanze von Marlin,
Martin Reichert

Publication management:
Sigrid Wollmeiner

Book editing:
Constanze von Marlin,
schmedding.vonmarlin.

Copyediting:
Dawn Michelle d'Atri

Translation:
Steven Lindberg
Rik Nys (pp. 193–203)

Design:
Heimann + Schwantes, Berlin

Printing and Binding:
Eberl & Kœsel GmbH & Co. KG,
Altusried-Krugzell

Publisher:
Deutscher Kunstverlag GmbH
Berlin München
Lützowstraße 33
10785 Berlin
www.deutscherkunstverlag.de

Part of Walter de Gruyter GmbH
Berlin Boston
www.degruyter.com

The German National Library
lists this publication in the
German National Bibliography;
detailed bibliographic data
are available on the Internet at
http://dnb.dnb.de.

www.smb.museum

ISBN 978-3-422-98652-7

Supported by Siemens

SIEMENS